Eyes Open 4

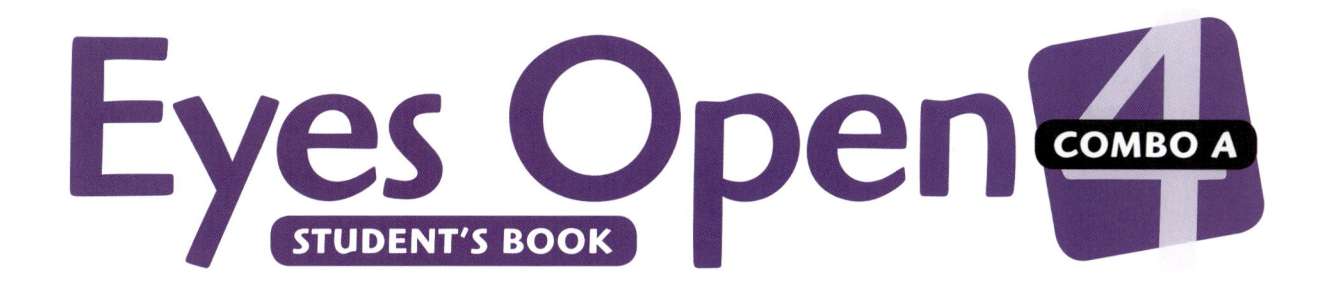

Student's Book

Combo A

Ben Goldstein & Ceri Jones
with Vicki Anderson

CAMBRIDGE UNIVERSITY PRESS

Discovery EDUCATION

Starter Unit	Vocabulary		Language focus	
	p4 -ed and -ing adjectives, Phrasal verbs **p5** Energy issues, make and do **p6** Art around us, Performing **p7** Adventure sports and activities, Survival essentials		**p4** Past simple vs. past continuous, Question words **p5** Present perfect and past simple, Present perfect with *still*, *yet*, *already* and *just* **p6** Word order in questions, Subject/object questions **p7** Present perfect with *ever*, *never*, *for* and *since*, Present perfect questions	

Unit	Vocabulary	Reading	Language focus 1	Listening and vocabulary
1 Trends	**p9** Clothes	**p10** Short online texts **Explore** words in context	**p11** *used to* and *would* **Get it right!** questions with *used to* ▶ Milan fashion week	**p12** An interview Adjectives and dependent prepositions
2 A helping hand	**p19** Personal qualities	**p20** A magazine article **Explore** word building	**p21** Reflexive pronouns and *each other* **Get it right!** reflexive pronouns ▶ Born to dive	**p22** A news report Phrasal verbs (learning and socialising)
	Review Unit 1 and 2 page 28–29			
3 Young achievers	**p31** Training and qualifications **Get it right!** *job* and *work*	**p32** A profile **Explore** expressions with *take*	**p33** *be going to* and present tenses for the future ▶ Insectmobile	**p34** A discussion Achievements
4 Fabulous food	**p41** Cooking verbs	**p42** Short online texts **Explore** words in context	**p43** First conditional with *if*, *when* and *unless* **Get it right!** *will* ▶ Oil from goats?	**p44** Adjectives describing food A game show
	Review Unit 3 and 4 page 50–51			

Project p123   Irregular verbs and phonemic script: Back of book

Language focus 2	Discover Culture (Video and Reading)	Speaking	Writing	Extras
p13 Past perfect **p96 Say it right!** Sentence stress in the past perfect	**p14** ▶ Inside the guitar **p15** A magazine article **Explore** compound nouns	**p16** ▶ **Real talk:** What music and fashion were your parents into when they were growing up? Buying clothes	**p17** A biography **Useful language:** Sequencers and connectors	**p115 CLIL** Social Science – The history of jeans ▶ Trendsetters **p99 Grammar reference** **p107 Vocabulary bank**
p23 Present perfect simple Present perfect continuous Present perfect simple vs. present perfect continuous **p96 Say it right!** Stress and intonation in questions with *How long?*	**p24** ▶ A very Indian wedding **p25** A blog post **Explore** words in context	**p26** ▶ **Real talk:** How have you helped a friend through a difficult situation? Showing concern	**p27** A personal email **Useful language:** Expressing how we feel	**p116 CLIL** Technology – The changing classroom ▶ The house of the future **p100 Grammar reference** **p108 Vocabulary bank**
p35 Predictions with *be going to*, *will* and *may/might* Future continuous **p96 Say it right!** Contracted forms in the future continuous	**p36** ▶ The young and the brave **p37** A newspaper article **Explore** words in context	**p38** ▶ **Real talk:** Are you saving up for something special? What? Making decisions	**p39** An opinion essay **Useful language:** Linking phrases	**p117 CLIL** Natural Science – The Archimedes' Principle ▶ A cool experiment **p101 Grammar reference** **p109 Vocabulary bank**
p45 Second conditional with *could* and *might* **p96 Say it right!** Stress and intonation in second conditional questions	**p46** ▶ Fruits of the sea **p47** An online article **Explore** prepositional phrases	**p48** ▶ **Real talk:** What would you make if you had to cook for your family for a day? Giving instructions	**p49** Describing a local dish **Useful language:** Cooking and eating	**p118 CLIL** Technology – Vertical farming ▶ You are what you eat **p102 Grammar reference** **p110 Vocabulary bank**

Starter Unit

Summer holidays
Past simple vs. past continuous

1 💬 Talk about the picture with your partner. Why do you think they are on the island?

2 🔊 **1.01** Listen to the story. Why were Pete and Maria on the island?

3 🔊 **1.01** Complete the text with the correct form of the past simple or past continuous. Then listen again and check.

Last summer, Pete and Maria ¹*went* (go) on a cruise holiday in the Caribbean with their parents. One day, the ship ² .... (sail) between some islands when it ³ .... (stop) and the captain said, 'You can all swim now.' Pete and Maria ⁴ .... (jump) in the water to look at the fish. While they ⁵ .... (swim), the wind ⁶ .... (push) them behind the ship. Suddenly, they ⁷ .... (see) some sharks coming towards them. They ⁸ .... (swim) as fast as possible to the nearest island. Then the ship ⁹ .... (begin) to sail away. They ¹⁰ .... (shout) for help. They could still see their parents, who ¹¹ .... (relax) on sunbeds on the deck!

Question words

4 Pete and Maria were rescued a week later. Complete the questions with the words in the box.

| why | ~~how~~ | when | who | which | where | what |

1 *How* did you feel when you got to the island?
2 .... did you see when you got there?
3 .... did you meet on the island?
4 .... animals did you see?
5 .... did you sleep?
6 .... did the helicopter come?
7 .... did they take so long to rescue you?

-ed and -ing adjectives, Phrasal verbs

5 🔊 **1.02** Choose the correct words to complete the answers to the interview questions in Exercise 4. Then listen and check.

Pete: When we got to the island, we were so ¹(tired)/ tiring!
Maria: We looked up and saw the ship ²setting off / picking up without us!
Pete: It was crazy! It was so ³worried / worrying! Then it started getting dark and we were ⁴terrified / terrifying!
Maria: But we were sure they would ⁵find out / come back for us soon. So we decided to ⁶look round / chill out the island and try to find some food.
Pete: The island wasn't very ⁷interested / interesting. There were no people and no animals. We found some fruit to eat. Then we slept under a tree until morning. Soon we were really ⁸bored / boring.
Maria: A week later, we saw a helicopter and they came to rescue us. We were so happy. But we still haven't ⁹found out / picked up why it took them so long!
Pete: We were so ¹⁰excited / exciting about being rescued that we didn't ask our parents how they forgot us!

Your turn

6 Ask and answer about a holiday. Use the words in the boxes to help you.

why	how
when	
who	which
where	what

interested	excited	tiring
boring	interesting	tired
worrying	exciting	bored
terrifying	worried	

Where did you go?

I went to Rome. It was really interesting. What about you?

I went to …

UNIT S

Home life
Energy issues

1 Match the verbs (1–6) with the phrases (a–f).

1 reduce *e*
2 don't waste
3 don't leave
4 save
5 turn down
6 switch off

a energy to save the planet
b the TV, computers and chargers when not using them
c water – have showers, not baths
d electrical appliances on standby at night
e the amount of rubbish you make by using less plastic
f heating and air conditioning whenever you can

Present perfect and past simple

2 🔊 1.03 Listen to Tina. Who is helping to save the planet?

3 🔊 1.03 Complete the text with the correct form of the present perfect or past simple. Then listen again and check.

We [1] *'ve reduced* (reduce) our electricity bills by 20% this year. Last year we [2] …. (spend) £500 but this year it's only £400. We [3] …. (save) lots of energy by turning the heating down when we go to bed. I also [4] …. (have) a shower last night instead of a bath so I [5] …. (not waste) lots of water! I [6] …. (stop) leaving my phone charger on standby too. Now I only switch it on when I'm charging it. Last night my dad [7] …. (leave) the TV on but I [8] …. (switch) it off! My mum [9] …. (buy) some reusable shopping bags, so from now on we will never use plastic ones. I think we are the greenest family in school.

Your turn

4 Use the phrases below to talk about your energy use.

- I save …
- I switch off …
- I don't waste …
- I reduce …
- I turn down …
- I don't leave …

I switch off my computer when I'm not using it.

make and do

5 Complete the sentences with *make* or *do*.

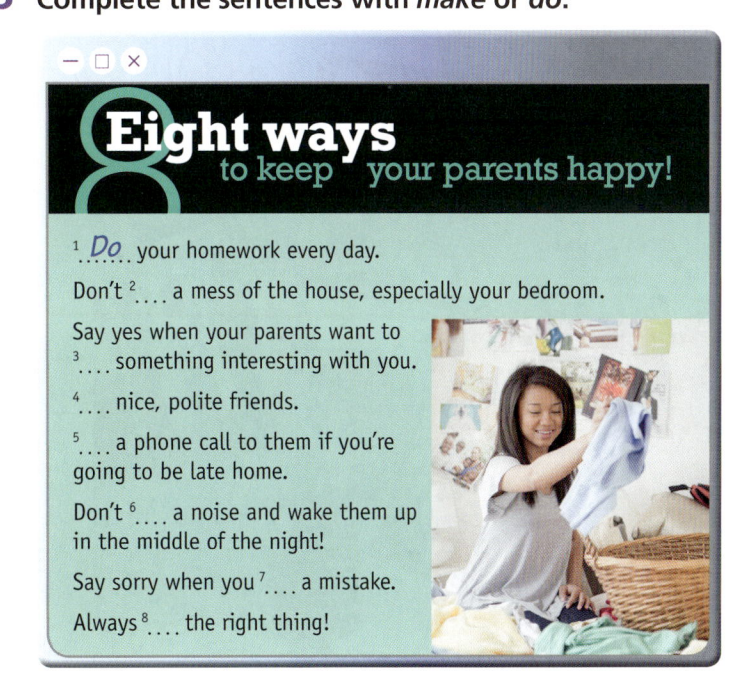

Eight ways to keep your parents happy!

[1] *Do* your homework every day.
Don't [2] …. a mess of the house, especially your bedroom.
Say yes when your parents want to [3] …. something interesting with you.
[4] …. nice, polite friends.
[5] …. a phone call to them if you're going to be late home.
Don't [6] …. a noise and wake them up in the middle of the night!
Say sorry when you [7] …. a mistake.
Always [8] …. the right thing!

Present perfect with *still*, *yet*, *already* and *just*

6 🔊 1.04 Listen to Tina and her mum. What is Tina doing? What has her mum done?

7 🔊 1.04 Choose the correct words. Then listen again and check.

Mum: Tina! Have you finished your Maths homework [1] **yet** / already?
Tina: No Mum, I've got lots of homework today. I haven't started my Maths [2] **yet** / **still**.
Mum: Really? So what have you done so far?
Tina: I've [3] **still** / **just** finished Science and now I'm going to start Geography. Then I [4] **already** / **still** have History and French to do. And Maths of course.
Mum: Right. I think you need all afternoon. I've [5] **already** / **just** made a cake. Do you want some?
Tina: No thanks. I've [6] **already** / **yet** had some chocolate today.

Your turn

8 Ask and answer questions about what you have done today.

Have you done your homework yet?
No, I haven't done it yet.
Have you already had lunch?
Yes, I have.

Arts and entertainment
Art around us

1 Match the pictures (a–h) with the words in the box.

> mural   portrait   orchestra   microphone
> gallery   exhibition   sculpture   juggler

Word order in questions

2 Put the words in order to make questions for a band, All for One.
1. playing / are / When / tonight / you / ?
   When are you playing tonight?
2. meet / you / did / How / all / ?
3. songs / writes / the / play / all / Who / you / ?
4. concert / When / first / was / your / ?
5. other / can / instruments / play / What / you / ?
6. do / do / you / your / in / time / What / free / ?
7. other / music / like / you / What / do / ?
8. going / after / finish / you / are / here / Where / you / ?

Performing

3 🔊 1.05 Listen to an interview with the band. Where did they meet?

4 🔊 1.05 Listen again and complete the notes.

> Concert starts at ¹ *8 pm* .
>
> Met at an arts festival – Simon and Tony were ² .... .
>
> Simon plays the ³ .... and the piano.
>
> Tony plays the violin and the ⁴ .... .
>
> John sings and likes painting ⁵ .... .
>
> First concert – two years ago – they've never played in a ⁶ .... like this.
>
> Free time – John does acting classes – he'd like to act ⁷ .... too.

Subject/object questions

5 Complete the questions.
1. 'Hi Simon! Who *is your favourite singer* ?'
   'My favourite singer is Lady Gaga.'
2. 'Boys! What .... ?'
   'We have pancakes for breakfast!'
3. 'Hey Tony! Who .... ?'
   'My uncle taught me to play!'
4. 'Hi there! What .... ?'
   'Lots of things give us ideas for songs – love, life, friends …'
5. 'Hey guys! Who .... ?'
   'We often listen to the Beatles!'
6. 'Dudes! What .... ?'
   'We chilled out in the hotel last night!'

Your turn

6 Work with a partner. Student A is a member of a band, Student B is a music journalist. Do an interview.

> Hi Joseph! So, what instruments can you play?

> I can play …

Exciting lives
Adventure sports and activities

1. **Put the letters in order to make adventure sports and activities.**
   1. I love ..*trekking*.. (gnirektk) – I can walk all day in the mountains and not get tired.
   2. We look forward to winter and snowy weather every year so we can go .... (nkisig).
   3. My parents taught me to swim when I was a boy so that I would be safe when we went .... (isaingl).
   4. You need very strong arms and no fear of high places if you want to try .... (bilcgnim).
   5. We saw all the big five animals when we went on .... (afairs) in Africa.
   6. People say the USA has the best .... (emeht prak) in the world, with the biggest and best rides!
   7. My first adventure holiday was a .... (rmumse pamc) in the mountains when I was 14.
   8. You can meet kids your age from another country if you go on a .... (locohs ganexhce).

Present perfect with *ever, never, for* and *since*

2. 🔊 1.06 **Listen to Sam. When did he start travelling?**

3. 🔊 1.06 **Choose the correct words to complete Sam's blog post about his travel experiences. Then listen again and check.**

Present perfect questions

4. **Complete the questions for Sam. Use the present perfect.**
   1. Sam, ..*have you ever been*.. (ever/go) to Antarctica?
   2. Hey Sam. How long .... (live) abroad?
   3. Hi mate. .... (finish packing/yet)?
   4. Dear Sam. How long .... (have) your blog?
   5. Wow, your trips are amazing! .... (ever/be) on TV?
   6. Hi Sam. I'd love to meet you. I live in Honolulu. .... (visit/Hawaii/yet)?

Survival essentials

5. **Match the words to make survival essentials.**
   1. sun *c*   a bottle
   2. water   b aid kit
   3. first   c cream
   4. pen-   d knife
   5. contact   e bag
   6. sleeping   f lenses

Your turn

6. **Imagine you are adventure travellers. Take turns to interview each other.**

   - Have you ever been sailing?
   - Yes, I've been sailing many times.
   - Where have you been to?

Sam around the world

I was born to travel! I've moved around the world every year ¹**ever / (since)** I was born! My parents took me on lots of trips when I was a child, and I've ²**always / never** lost the love of travelling. I started travelling full-time when I left school, and now I've been an adventure traveller ³**for / since** ten years. I've been to most of the continents, but I've ⁴**never / always** been to Australia. I've wanted to go there ⁵**from / for** years. That's my next trip! Have you ⁶**ever / never** been there? Follow my blog as I explore the biggest country in the world!

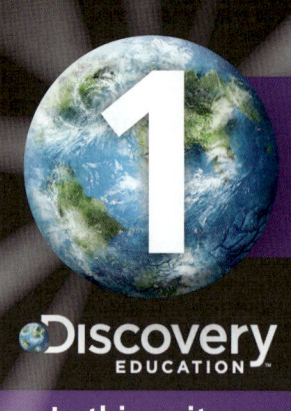

1 Trends

Discovery EDUCATION

In this unit ...

- Milan fashion week **p11** 
- Inside the guitar **p14** 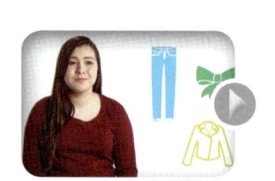
- Music and fashion **p16** 
- CLIL Trendsetters **p115**

Vocabulary
- Clothes
- Words in context
- Adjectives and dependent prepositions
- Compound nouns

Language focus
- *used to* and *would*
- Past perfect

Unit aims
I can ...
- talk about the kind of clothes I like to wear.
- understand short online texts about fashions and an article about style icons.
- talk about past habits and experiences.
- understand a radio interview with an actor.
- buy clothes in a shop.
- write a short biography of a famous person.

BE CURIOUS

What can you see in the photo?
Start thinking
- Where is the girl? What is she doing?
- What do you like doing with your friends in your free time?
- How is this different from what your parents like doing?

Vocabulary Clothes

1 🔊 **1.07** Match the phrases in the box with the clothes (a–j) in the pictures. Then listen, check and repeat.

> a leather jacket   a stripy shirt   a silk scarf   a cool T-shirt   flat shoes   tight jeans
> a flowery dress   a denim skirt   a baggy jumper   a fitted coat

2 Look again at the phrases in Exercise 1. Find words that describe:
  a the material the clothes are made from
  b the pattern on the material
  c the size or shape
  d a personal opinion about the clothes

3 🔊 **1.08** Listen to three people talking about the clothes they are wearing. Find the people in the pictures.

Your turn

4 Look again at the phrases in Exercise 1. Change the adjectives to create new phrases to describe clothes you like wearing.

*leather jacket – denim jacket,
tight jeans – baggy jeans*

5 Ask and answer with your partner.
  1 Which of the clothes in the pictures and in Exercise 4 do you have in your wardrobe?
  2 How often do you wear them?
  3 What kind of clothes do you like wearing? Why?
  4 Do your parents ever tell you what to wear? When? Are you happy to wear the clothes they suggest?

> In my wardrobe, I've got a really baggy jumper. It's horrible!

> Me too! My aunt gave it me for my birthday but I never wear it.

➡ **Vocabulary bank** • page 107

Reading Short online texts

1 Read the introduction to the quiz and look at the photos. Can you answer the questions?

QUIZ TEENAGE FASHIONS from the past

How much do you know about teenage fashions? Test yourself with our quick fashion quiz. Look at the photos.
- What order do they come in, from the earliest to the most recent?
- What did the different groups use to call themselves? Can you remember their names?

2 🔊 **1.09** Read the text and check your answers.

A Teddy boys and girls first appeared on the streets of Britain in the 1950s. They loved rock and roll music and they used to dress like the American teenagers in rock and roll movies. The boys wore long jackets and tight trousers. They wore their hair long at the front. They would put a lot of gel in it and wear it in a quiff. The girls used to wear wide skirts and high ponytails.

B The hippy fashion started in the late 1960s. It was a very relaxed style and very different from the formal clothes Teds used to wear. Hippies wore loose clothes, with colourful flowery patterns. Men had long hair and beards. Women had long hair too and they used to wear long scarves and Indian jewellery. Sometimes they would paint flowers on their hands and faces.

C The first punks appeared on the streets of London in the late 1970s. They didn't use to spend a lot of money on clothes. Their favourite colour was black. They wore tight trousers with holes and baggy T-shirts with offensive words and expressions on them. They had dyed hair – pink or green or blue – and they used to wear dog collars as necklaces and safety-pins as earrings. They wanted to shock people and break the rules.

D This colourful, creative style started in the early 1980s. New Romantics loved unusual clothes that often looked like costumes from a pirate film and both girls and boys used to wear extravagant make-up. Their fashion was a reaction to the dark side of punk.

FACT! *81% of teens get their ideas for clothes and fashion from friends and classmates and not from magazines or TV.*

3 Read the text again. Complete the sentences with Teds, Hippies, Punks or New Romantics.
1 *Punks* didn't like rules.
2 …. copied a style from another country.
3 The style of both …. and …. developed in reaction to earlier fashions.
4 …. and …. wore clothes with lots of colour.
5 …. and …. had special hairstyles.
6 …. and …. wore tight trousers.
7 …. wanted to look like characters they saw in films.
8 …. were influenced by nature.

🔍 Explore words in context

4 Find the words in the text and then look for examples in the photos. Which ones can you see?

> quiff   ponytail   loose clothes
> dyed hair   dog collar   safety-pins
> extravagant make-up

Your turn

5 Ask and answer with your partner.
1 Are any of these fashions still common in your country? If yes, which? Who wears them?
2 What styles are common among young people today? Do you like them? Why/Why not?

UNIT 1

3 🔊 **1.10** Look at your answers in Exercise 2. Which verbs can you use with *would*? Then listen and check.

👁 Get it right!
To form questions, use *did* + *use to* + infinitive.
Did you **use to** have a quiff, Dad? ✓
~~Did you used to have … ?~~ ✗

4 Write questions with *used to*. Add three more questions using your own ideas.
1 you / walk to school on your own?
Did you use to walk to school on your own?
2 you / do any sports?
3 you / wear a uniform?
4 your teachers / give you a lot of homework?
5 Who / you / play with in the playground?

🟥 Your turn

5 Think about when you were nine. Ask and answer the questions in Exercise 4 with your partner.

> Did you use to walk to school on your own?

> Well … I used to walk to school with my mum, but sometimes I would walk home alone.

6 Is your life very different now? Use *used to* and *would* and write sentences to describe the differences between your life now and when you were nine.
When I was nine, I used to spend a lot of time with my parents, now I spend more time with my friends.

Language focus 1
used to and *would*

1 Complete the examples from the text. Then choose the correct words to complete the rules.

used to	
+	Both boys and girls ¹…. to wear extravagant make-up.
–	They ²…. to spend a lot of money on clothes.
?	What ³…. the different groups …. to call themselves? **Did** you **use to be** a hippy? Yes, I **did**. No, I **didn't**.

would	
+	They ⁴…. put a lot of gel in it. They ⁵…. paint flowers on their hands and faces. **Would** he **break** the rules? Yes, he **would**. No, he **wouldn't**.

- We use *used to* and *would* to talk about **single events in the past / past habits**.
- We only use *used to / would* with actions. We use *used to / would* with actions, states and feelings (*be, have, live, love, want, care*, etc.).

➡ **Grammar reference** • page 99

2 Complete the text with the correct form of *used to*. Use the verbs in brackets.

When my dad was a student, he ¹…. (be) a New Romantic. He and his friends ²…. (go) to concerts together all the time. They ³…. (like) wearing really extravagant clothes. They ⁴…. (dress) as pirates and paint their faces. He ⁵…. (have) long, blond hair, but then he started working in a bank in the city and he ⁶…. (not go out) so much. He forgot about all the things he ⁷…. (love) doing with his friends. Now he looks completely different!

Learn about fashion shows and being a top model.
- What do you know about Milan?
- Do you know the names of any famous Italian designers?
- Would you like to work as a catwalk model? Why/Why not?

Discovery EDUCATION
1.1 Milan fashion week

Listening An interview

1 Work with a partner. Look at the photos and the poster and answer the questions.
   1 Do you know anything about the film?
   2 What do you think is the connection between the film and the two photos?
   3 How has the world changed in the last 30 years?

2 🔊 1.11 Listen to an interview with a young actor, David, who is taking part in a theatre production of the film. Check your answers.

3 🔊 1.11 Listen again and choose the correct options.
   1 The film first came out in **1980 / 1985**.
   2 In the film, Marty travels from the **1950s to the 1980s / 1980s to the 1950s**.
   3 In the theatre production, Marty travels from 2015 to the **1980s / 1950s**.
   4 The theatre production focuses on life **now / in the past**.
   5 David's parents were teenagers in the **1950s / 1980s**.
   6 Teenagers **were / weren't** interested in the same things in the 1980s as they are now.
   7 There **were / weren't** any touchscreens in the 1980s.
   8 The presenter **has / hasn't** seen the show.

Your turn

4 Ask and answer with your partner.
   1 Would you like to see the film or the show? Why/Why not?
   2 Would you like to travel back in time to see your parents when they were teenagers?
   3 Do you think their lives were very different from yours? If yes, in what way?

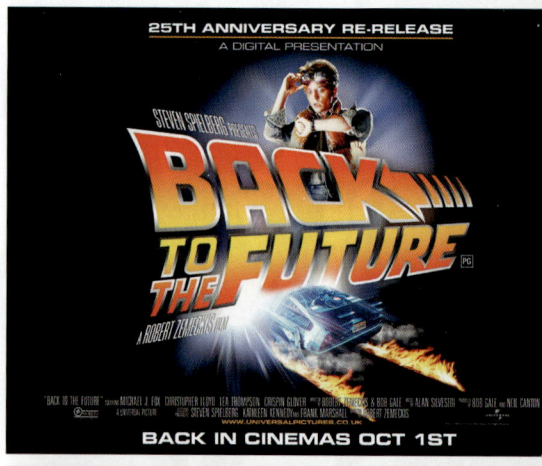

Vocabulary Adjectives and dependent prepositions

5 🔊 1.12 Choose the correct prepositions to complete the sentences from the interview. Then listen and check.
   1 I was really excited (about) / in working on the show.
   2 I'm fascinated **about / by** that side of the show …
   3 … what teenagers were interested **of / in** then …
   4 … teenagers were keen **by / on** the same things, like …
   5 … some people have been a little disappointed **by / of** the show.
   6 … we're really happy **in / with** it …
   7 … and proud **of / on** all our hard work.
   8 We aren't afraid **in / of** criticism you know!

Your turn

6 Write five sentences that you think are true for your partner. Use some of the adjectives and prepositions from Exercise 5.
   I think you were disappointed by the result of the football match last night.

7 Work with a partner. Ask and answer questions to find out if the sentences you wrote in Exercise 6 are correct.

> Were you disappointed by the result of the football match last night?

> No, I wasn't! My team won 3–0!

Vocabulary bank • page 107

Language focus 2 Past perfect

1 Complete the examples from the listening on page 12. Then answer the questions in the box.

> had   hadn't (x2)   seen   thought

+	I **had** always **wanted** to be in a big show.
–	I ¹…. really …. about it before.
?	²…. you …. it before you started on the production? Yes, I **had seen** it twice. No, I ³…. **seen** it.

> 1 What do you use the past perfect to talk about?
>   a an action that happened before another action
>   b an action that happened after another action
> 2 Which tense do you use to talk about the most recent of two past actions?
>   a the past simple   b the past perfect

➡ **Grammar reference** • page 99

2 Choose the correct form of the verbs in the sentences below.
1 My brother **told** / **had told** me about a new band yesterday. I **didn't hear** / **hadn't heard** of them before.
2 When I got to the party last night, Jo **went** / **had gone** home, so I **didn't see** / **hadn't seen** her.
3 We went to a great burger bar last weekend. I **wasn't** / **hadn't been** there before. The food **was** / **had been** really good.
4 I **arrived** / **'d arrived** late for football last week, the match **started** / **had started** when I got there and the coach didn't let me play!

3 💬 Work with a partner. Look at the pictures and tell the story using the verbs in the box. Can you use all the verbs?

> get on   not let   wait   have   want   sell out   ask
> say   put up their tents   see   arrive   be

> The concert last night was absolutely fantastic …

4 🔊 **1.13** Complete the text with the correct form of the past simple or past perfect. Use the verbs in Exercise 3. Then listen and check.

The concert last night ¹…. absolutely fantastic. We ²…. to see the band for a very long time, so when we ³…. a poster of the concert two months ago at a bus stop, we were very excited. We ⁴…. our parents if we could go and they ⁵…. yes! They ⁶…. us go to a concert on our own before and we were really excited.

A month later, we ⁷…. a train to go and buy the tickets. We ⁸…. at the ticket office the night before with a tent. A lot of other people ⁹…. on the street before us. The next day we ¹⁰…. for five hours until at last we ¹¹…. the tickets in our hands. Five minutes later, all the tickets ¹²…. ! We were so lucky! And the concert was brilliant.

➡ **Say it right!** • page 96

Your turn

5 Make notes about the first time you did or saw something special.

first One Direction concert – never been to a live concert before – totally amazing!

6 Work with a partner. Ask and answer these questions about your experience. Add more questions using your own ideas. Were your experiences similar?
1 What was your experience and when did you do it?
2 Did you know anyone who had had a similar experience before?
3 How long had you waited for it to happen?
4 Was it as good as you'd expected?
5 How did you feel?

> I went to a One Direction concert last summer. My sister had been but I had never …

Discover Culture

1 💬 Work with a partner. Look at the photos. What's the main difference between the two guitars? What do they have in common?

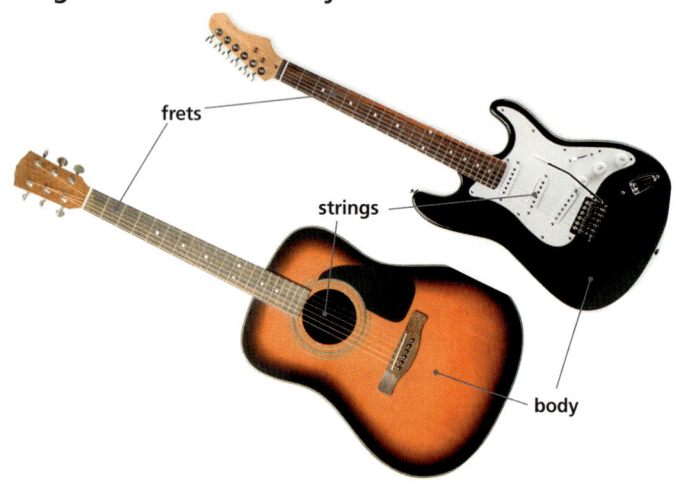

frets
strings
body

2 💬 Work with a partner. Discuss these questions.
1. In what kind of places can you see the two different types of guitar?
2. What kind of people do you associate with each type of guitar?
   Traditional guitar: classical musician …
   Electric guitar: pop star …

Find out about how guitars are made.

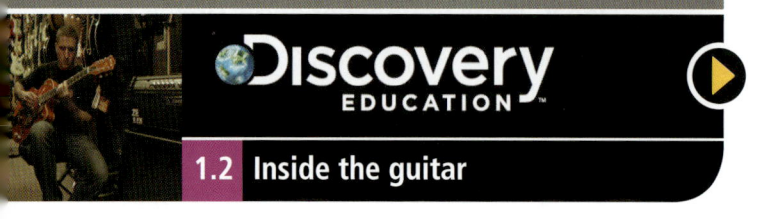

Discovery EDUCATION
1.2 Inside the guitar

3 ▶ 1.2 Watch the video. What is the main focus?
a The history of both types of guitars
b How an electric guitar works
c How an electric guitar is made

4 Test your memory. Can you answer the questions?
1. Which type of guitar is shown first?
2. Where do we first see traditional guitars?
3. Which kind of guitar is produced in the factory?
4. What part of the guitar is made by machines?
5. Which parts are added by hand?
6. What do we see in the last shot?

5 ▶ 1.2 Watch the video again and check your answers.

6 Look at the diagram. Can you explain how an electric guitar works?
They put magnets under the strings. The magnets …

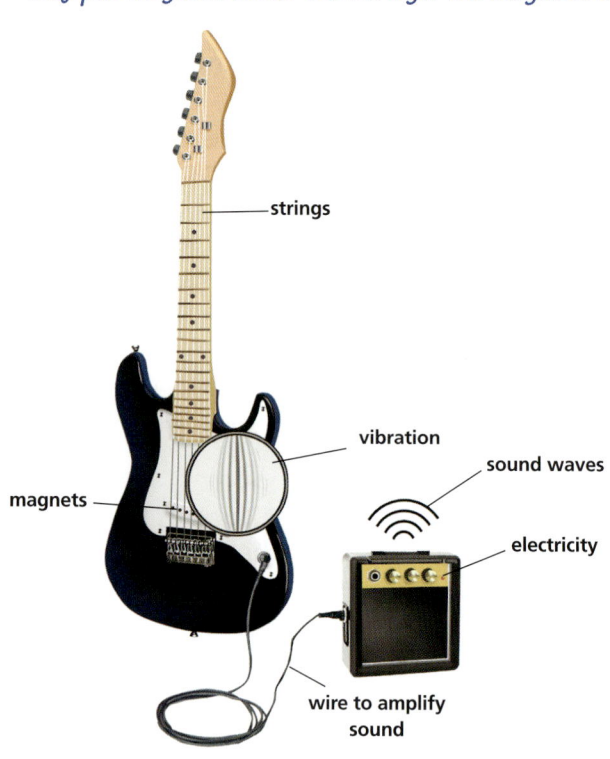

strings
vibration
sound waves
magnets
electricity
wire to amplify sound

7 ▶ 1.2 Watch the video from 02.10 to 02.37 and check your answers.

Your turn

8 Ask and answer with your partner.
1. Do you play the guitar or know anyone who plays the guitar? What type of guitar do they play?
2. Do you often see people playing the guitar, or other musical instruments, on the street in your town?
3. Have you ever learned to play an instrument? If yes, what and why? Do you still play it? If no, which instrument would you like to learn to play? Why?

Retro BRITAIN

There are lots of icons which represent the UK but some only symbolise the Britain of the past …

THE BEATLES

The 'Fab Four', the most popular guitar band of all time, are known and loved all over the world! They released their first album more than 50 years ago but their songs are still as popular as ever. The band went through a number of style changes over the years from 1959 to 1970, but this image of the young band in their cool suits and short hairstyles is probably the most iconic.

THE RED TELEPHONE BOX

The first telephone box was designed in the 1920s, when very few people had telephones at home. People don't use them anymore, but they still decorate some street corners, especially in tourist areas. You used to put a penny into it to make a call. In the 1930s, domestic phones appeared but they didn't have a keypad like modern phones, in fact they looked something like this. People used to get tired of dialling the numbers!

THE MINI

In 1959, the most famous car in the British motor industry arrived: the Mini! It was a car popular with both the rich and the famous – everybody loved the Mini. Before production stopped in 2000, nearly six million people had bought one! Now there is a new Mini on the streets, but it's not British anymore – it's German! The first Mini cost just £500. The new German Mini can cost as much as £16,000!

THE BLACK CAB

The London cab is the icon that has survived the longest, but, of course, the design has changed a lot! The first cabs, introduced in the 17th century, were pulled by horses. Although traditionally black, they also come in other colours, including gold! Nowadays more and more cabs are being covered all over in advertising. Today, you can also travel in them in other world cities but it will cost you a little more than the original taxi fare of sixpence!

FACT! There used to be 80,000 red telephone boxes in the UK, but there aren't many of them left now.

Reading A magazine article

1 Work with a partner. Look at the photos. What do they show? Do you think all these things are still common or popular in the UK?

2 🔊 1.16 Read the magazine article and check your answers.

3 Read the article again. What do the four icons have in common?
   a Their appearance has changed a lot over time.
   b They are all icons from the 20th century.
   c They've all survived as icons for at least 50 years.

Explore compound nouns

4 Match words from box A with words from box B to form compound nouns. Then find the compound nouns in the text and check your answers.
   guitar band

   A ~~guitar~~ style telephone street motor taxi

   B box corners ~~band~~ industry fare changes

5 Which words from the list do not combine with the words in bold to form compound nouns?
   1 **guitar**: string, ~~bag~~, music
   2 **style**: icon, consultant, model
   3 **telephone**: call, number, name
   4 **street**: house, art, fashion
   5 **motor**: show, vehicle, driver
   6 **taxi**: cab, driver, call

➡ Vocabulary bank • page 107

Your turn

6 Ask and answer with your partner.
   1 What people or objects are icons in your country?
   2 When did they first become popular?
   3 Are they still popular nowadays?
   4 Do you think they are positive symbols of your country and culture? Why/Why not?

   I think the most famous pop group is probably …

   On the streets in my country, there are lots of …

Speaking Buying clothes

Real talk: What music and fashion were your parents into when they were growing up?

1 ▶ 1.3 Watch or listen to the teenagers. Match the sentences (1–6) with the music or people in the box.

> disco   the Beatles   punk   Michael Jackson   classical and pop   no music

1 My parents liked really different things.
2 They were more into fashion, especially my mum.
3 There are no photos, so I don't really know.
4 My grandmother still remembers seeing a famous group.
5 They still listen to the music and do the dances!
6 They looked the same and wore the same clothes.

2 💬 What music and fashion are *you* into? Ask and answer with your partner.

3 🔊 1.17 Listen to Olivia and her friend Raquel. What does Olivia buy?

4 Complete the conversation with the useful language.

Useful language

How about this top?
You look great!
Where are the changing rooms?
They're my size, too.
Do you think the top suits me?
They don't fit very well.

5 🔊 1.17 Listen again and check your answers.

6 💬 Work with a partner. Practise the conversation in Exercise 4.

7 💬 Work with a partner. Plan your own conversation. Use the ideas below and Exercise 4 to help you.

Olivia:	Right, I'm looking for a top for your party, and maybe a pair of jeans.
Raquel:	OK. ¹ *How about this top* ? You look good in purple.
Olivia:	Yes, it's really pretty. Oh, *these* are nice jeans and ² …. , too. This style is in at the moment. What do you think?
Raquel:	Mmm. I'm not so sure. Why don't you try them on?
Olivia:	OK. Where ³ …. ?
Raquel:	Over there on the right. Come on!
Olivia:	So, do you think ⁴ …. ?
Raquel:	Yes, you ⁵ …. !
Olivia:	Yes, I like it too, and it's half price. I think I'll get it.
Raquel:	What about the jeans?
Olivia:	They don't suit me, and they don't ⁶ …. . They're a bit tight.
Raquel:	Yeah, I see what you mean. What a shame!
Olivia:	Never mind, maybe we'll see some in the next shop.
Raquel:	You're joking! I think I've had enough!

You want to buy a new shirt, blouse or top for an end-of-school party. You look good in blue.

You want to buy a new pair of jeans or trousers for the school disco next weekend. You prefer black.

Writing A biography

1 Look at the photo and read the biography. Who are they and when were they popular?

1 The Swedish group ABBA formed in 1972. Björn and Benny had been in another band, but started their own group and asked their girlfriends, Agnetha and Anni-Frid, to join. The name ABBA came from the initials of their first names. Later on both couples got married.

2 ABBA became internationally famous when they won the Eurovision Song Contest in 1974 with *Waterloo*. Over the next eight years they became one of the most successful pop groups ever. They had many hits, including *Dancing Queen* and *SOS*. They had 22 number 1 records around the world. During that time they played pop and disco, and were famous for their glam-rock stage costumes. Although they used to sing in English, they also released two albums in Spanish. After selling millions of records, ABBA finally split up in 1982.

3 In the last few years their music has become popular again with the musical (and film) *Mamma Mia!* As a result, ABBA have now sold 380 million records!

2 Read the biography again and complete the fact file.

FACT FILE

The name of the group/artist: ¹ ....
Where they were from: ² ....
When they formed / split up: ³ .... / ....
When and where they were successful: ⁴ ....
Famous songs/albums: ⁵ ....
Type of music: ⁶ ....
Style of clothes/hair: ⁷ ....
Record sales: ⁸ ....
Personal facts about them: ⁹ ....
Unusual facts: ¹⁰ ....

3 Read the biography again and identify which paragraph the information in Exercise 2 is in.

Useful language

Sequencers and connectors
Use different phrases to show the sequence of events and the connection between pieces of information.
- *Although* they ... , they also ...
- *Over the next* eight years ...
- *After* selling millions of records ...
- *As a result*, ABBA have now sold ...

4 Look at the Useful language box. Find three other similar phrases in the biography in Exercise 1.

5 Complete the sentences with the phrases in the box.

> as a result   over the next   after   the last few years   although

1 .... ABBA were a pop group, they also had disco hits.
2 ABBA donated the song *Chiquitita* to UNICEF. It reached number 1 in ten countries and, ..., made a lot of money for the charity.
3 .... making records in Spanish, ABBA became popular in South America.
4 .... few years, they recorded lots of singles in Spanish.
5 In .... the musical *Mamma Mia!* has been on in the West End of London.

Get writing

PLAN

6 Plan a biography about a band or artist from the past.
- Use the headings in Exercise 2 and make notes.
- Think about what to put in each paragraph. Use Exercise 3 to help you.
- Find any information you need on the Internet or speak to older family members.

WRITE

7 Write your biography. Use your notes from Exercise 6 and the model text to help you.

CHECK

8 Can you say YES to these questions?
- Have you included all the information from Exercise 2 and at least one unusual fact?
- Have you used phrases to sequence events and show the connection between pieces of information?

UNIT 1

2 A helping hand

Discovery EDUCATION

In this unit ...

- Born to dive p21
- A very Indian wedding p24 
- Helping a friend p26 
- CLIL The house of the future p116 

Vocabulary
- Personal qualities
- Word building
- Phrasal verbs (learning and socialising)
- Words in context

Language focus
- Reflexive pronouns and *each other*
- Present perfect simple and present perfect continuous

Unit aims
I can ...
- talk about a person's qualities.
- understand a magazine article and a blog post about people and their lives.
- talk about things I've done and things happening in my life.
- understand a news report about an educational project.
- show concern.
- write a personal email.

BE CURIOUS

What can you see in the photo?
Start thinking
- What do you think the two pandas are trying to do? Why?
- What other animals sometimes help each other? How?
- Do you ever help people to do things? What kinds of things?

Vocabulary Personal qualities

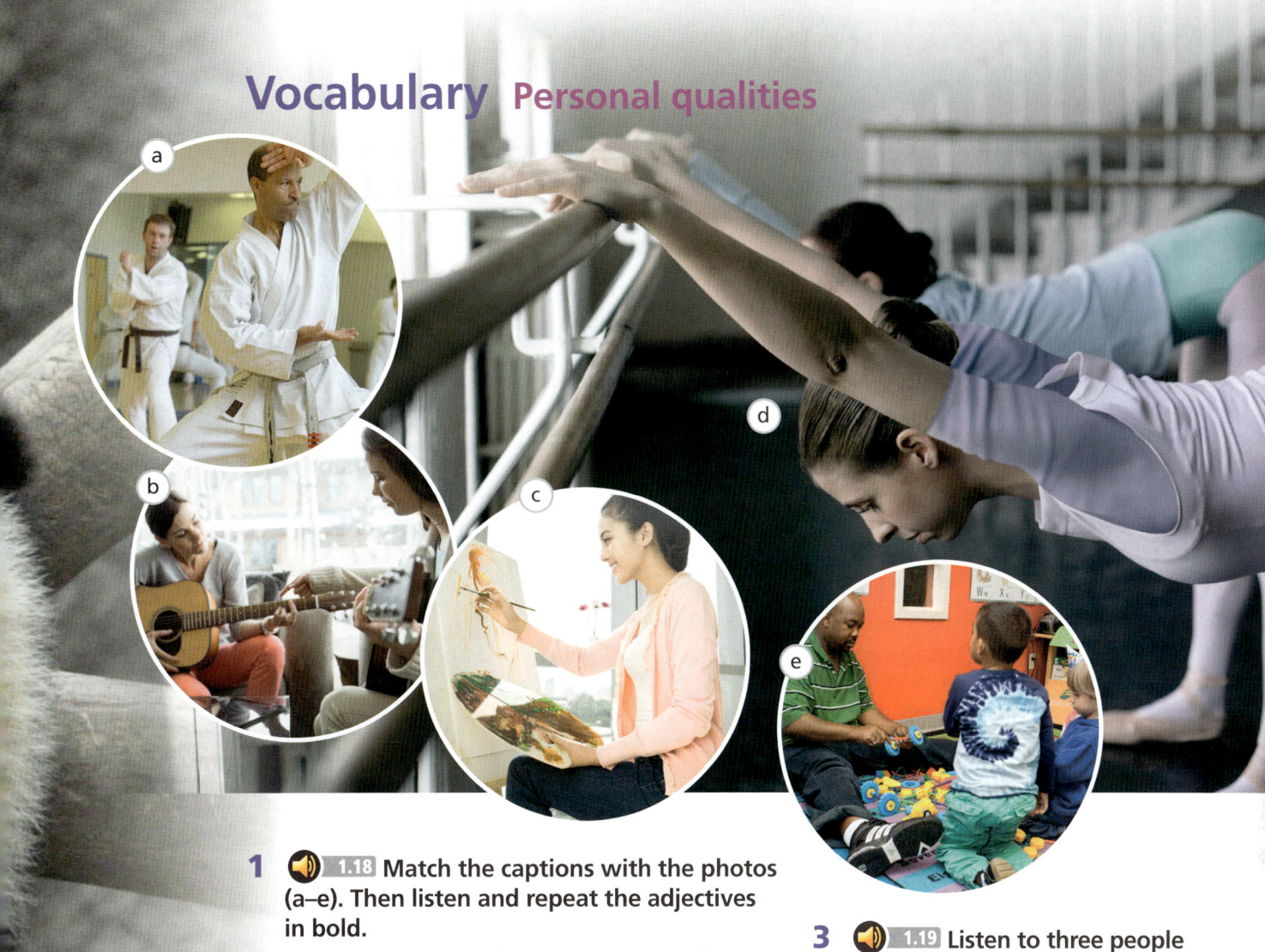

1 🔊 **1.18** Match the captions with the photos (a–e). Then listen and repeat the adjectives in bold.

1 She's very **talented**. Her pictures are really beautiful. And she's **determined** too. She tries again and again until she gets it just right.
2 He's great fun, he's so **sociable** he talks happily with everyone, but he's really good with the **shy** kids too – the ones who don't want to talk.
3 He's **strict** and he makes everyone in his class work hard, but they love him and are very **motivated**.
4 She's **passionate about** dancing. She loves it! And she's very **hard-working** too. She spends all her free time at the dance studio.
5 She's very **easy-going**. She never gets angry or **impatient** if I'm late or I haven't practised.

2 Match the sentences below to adjectives in Exercise 1.

1 'I don't like meeting new people, I never know what to say.'
2 'I absolutely love tennis, I think it's the best sport in the world!'
3 'I never let my students speak during the lesson. They have to listen and do what I say!'
4 'I really want to win this competition and I'm going to do everything I can to make it happen!'
5 'I get up at five o'clock every morning and go swimming for three hours before school.'
6 'I really hate it when people are late and they keep me waiting!'

3 🔊 **1.19** Listen to three people talking about a person who helps or teaches them. What adjectives are used to describe them?

1 Krista: *never impatient, …*
2 Steff:
3 Toni:

Your turn

4 Think of a person who helps you in some way. Write three sentences about him/her using adjectives from Exercise 1.

My big sister is very impatient. She always gets angry with me when I'm late.

5 Work with a partner. Discuss your descriptions in Exercise 4. Try to find three similarities between them.

> Maria's friend Lucy and my cousin Jenny are similar. They are both … And they both like …

➡ **Vocabulary bank** • page 108

A NATURAL BORN CLIMBER

Brooke Raboutou has just turned 12 and, with seven world records, is one of the best rock climbers in the world. One of her coaches explains that she's so good because she has really strong fingers and the incredible flexibility of a child. That helps her a lot and means she can do things older climbers have never dreamed of doing.

Brooke comes from a climbing family. Both her parents are past climbing champions. Her father stopped climbing some years ago, but her mother, Robyn, who won four world cup titles four years in a row, is still climbing. She runs a club for young climbers in Colorado, USA and coaches Brooke and her teammates. Sometimes it's difficult for mother and daughter to work together so closely, but they really respect and trust each other and Brooke says her mum is a great coach. Brooke says that her mother gives her a lot of good advice and is a very important part of her climbing life. Robyn can be strict, but she is also passionate about climbing, and she passes this passion on to her students.

Robyn says Brooke is very determined and is very good at motivating herself. This helps her when she's facing the challenges of this difficult sport. She is also very hard-working. Success in rock climbing is something you have to work at. To be a world-class athlete of any kind, you have to push yourself and train hard and that's what Brooke does, every day, at the club and at home. Brooke says that climbing is always there in their lives. They even have a climbing wall in their house!

But climbing isn't only hard work. It's fun too. Brooke loves climbing and when she's on a high rock, she feels happy. Strangely, she says that when she looks down, she isn't scared. All she does is think how cool it is to be so small compared to the rock.

FACT! The most difficult climb in the world is a 55-metre climb in a cave in Norway, created in 2013 by 20-year-old Czech climber Adam Ondra.

Reading A magazine article

1 💬 Work with a partner. Look at the headline for the article and the photo of Brooke and her mum. Choose two personal qualities to describe each of them.

2 🔊 1.20 Read the article and check your answers. How does Brooke feel about rock climbing? Why?

3 Read the article again and find information about:
1. what makes Brooke a good climber
2. Brooke's family and their connection to climbing
3. Brooke's relationship with her mum
4. what Brooke's mum does
5. why Brooke thinks her mum's good at her job
6. Brooke's thoughts when she's high up on a rock

Explore word building

4 Copy and complete the table with words from the article.

noun	adjective
¹*flexibility*	flexible
²	passionate
determination	³
⁴	challenging
⁵	successful
happiness	⁶

5 Write three sentences about world-class sportspeople using words from Exercise 4.

You need to be very determined if you want to be a successful sportsperson.

➔ Vocabulary bank • page 108

Your turn

6 Make notes about the questions.
1. What do you think are your best qualities?
2. Are there any qualities you don't have, but you'd really like to have? Why?

7 Ask and answer the questions in Exercise 6 with your partner. Are you similar?

> Well … I think I'm sociable and hard-working. What about you?

> That's difficult, I think …

Language focus 1 Reflexive pronouns and *each other*

1 Complete the examples from the text.
1. They really respect and trust .... .
2. Brooke is very determined and is very good at motivating .... .
3. To be a world-class athlete of any kind, you have to push .... and train hard.

2 Look again at the examples in Exercise 1. Copy and complete the table and answer the questions.

subject pronoun	object pronoun	reflexive pronoun
I	me	myself
you	you	¹.... /yourselves
he	him	himself
she	her	²....
it	it	itself
we	us	ourselves
they	them	themselves

1. In sentence 1, who does Brooke trust? And who does her mother trust?
2. In sentence 2, who motivates Brooke?
3. In sentence 3, who pushes a world-class climber to work harder?

➔ **Grammar reference** • page 100

3 Match the beginnings and the ends of the sentences.
1. She looked at herself *c*
2. They looked at each other
3. She's very independent and
4. The two sisters are great friends and
5. My best friend moved away last year and I really miss her but
6. He walked quickly down the street,
7. We work really well together and
8. Before an important climb, I always sit quietly on my own

a. she always looks after herself.
b. talking quietly to himself.
c. in the mirror as she practised her moves.
d. we talk to each other online every day.
e. and try to focus myself on the challenge.
f. help each other to focus on our strengths.
g. across the busy room and smiled.
h. they always look after each other.

👁 Get it right!
We write reflexive pronouns as one word.
yourself, themselves ✓
your self, them selves ✗
But we write *each other* as two words.
each other ✓   *eachother* ✗

4 🔊 **1.21** Complete the conversations with reflexive pronouns or *each other*. Then listen and check.
1. **A:** How's Matías? Did you see *each other* over the weekend?
   B: No, he's really busy preparing .... for the world championship. I never see him!
2. **A:** Did you ever ask .... why you love climbing so much?
   B: No, never, it's just part of me. But I do sometimes ask .... why I have to get out of bed so early to train every morning!
3. **A:** Did you and your family enjoy .... at the competition last week?
   B: Yes, it was great. My mum and my uncle hadn't seen .... for ages. It was really nice for them to be able to spend some time together.
4. **A:** Is Philly in school today? We were supposed to be seeing .... at lunchtime.
   B: She isn't here today. She hurt .... climbing.

Your turn

5 When was the last time you did these things? Make notes.
- hurt yourself
- taught yourself to do something new
- enjoyed yourself so much you didn't notice time passing
- found yourself in a difficult situation

6 Work with a partner. Discuss your ideas from Exercise 5.

> I hurt myself quite badly last weekend when I fell off my bike.

Learn about free diving.
- What do you know about free diving? What does it involve?
- What are the challenges?
- What qualities are important for a free diver?

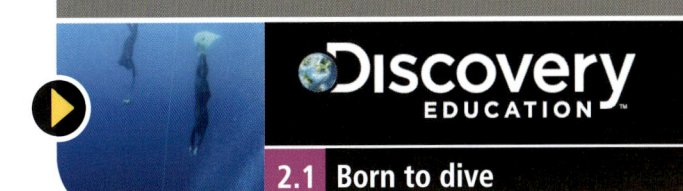

Discovery EDUCATION

2.1 Born to dive

Listening A news report

1 💬 **Work with a partner. Look at the photo and answer the questions.**
1. Who are the people in the photo?
2. What are they doing?
3. Who is helping who? How are they helping each other?

2 🔊 1.22 **Listen to a news report and check your answers.**

3 🔊 1.22 **Read the article about the project. Then listen again and find five more mistakes.**

> A great new project started at a Nottingham ~~primary~~ *secondary* school at the beginning of October. Once a month, older people from the community come to the school to learn how to use the Internet and their mobile phones. The same people come every time. So far they've all learned to share photos on their phones and set up a Facebook page. The students are great teachers, but sometimes they're a little impatient! 'Sometimes their explanations are too difficult!' said one of the older people on the course. The teenagers are really enjoying the chance to help people in their community.

Your turn

4 Discuss the questions in groups.
1. Do you think these classes could work in your school? Why/Why not?
2. Have you ever taught someone older than you how to use new technology? Was it difficult?

Vocabulary Phrasal verbs (learning and socialising)

5 🔊 1.23 **Match the phrasal verbs (1–8) with the definitions (a–h). Then listen and repeat the phrasal verbs in bold.**

1. A special project is **bringing together** students and older people.
2. More and more people are **signing up** every week.
3. We don't want them to think it's too difficult and **give up**.
4. They trust us and you know, **look up to** us in a way.
5. I've **set up** a Facebook page.
6. Do you **get on with** your teachers?
7. They're really good at **passing on** their knowledge.
8. We can always **count on** them to explain things simply and patiently.

a depend on someone
b have a good relationship with someone
c create something new
d stop doing something
e teach or give new information
f respect someone
g join a class or other organised activity
h help people be friendly to each other

6 Make notes about two people and two things from the list below.
- somebody you … *look up to / get on with / can count on when you have a problem*
- something in your life that you've … *given up / set up / passed on your knowledge of / signed up for*

7 💬 **Work with a partner. Discuss your ideas from Exercise 6.**

> I signed up for karate classes, but I didn't really enjoy it and after a month I gave up.

➡ **Vocabulary bank** • page 108

UNIT 2

Language focus 2
Present perfect simple

1 Look at the examples from the listening on page 22 and answer the questions.
- I**'ve learned** a lot of things since we started.
- We**'ve had** five meetings since September.

> 1 Do they refer to a time period that has finished?
> 2 Do they describe a single action or a series of actions?
> 3 Can we use the present perfect simple to say how many?

➡ **Grammar reference** • page 100

2 Write questions using the prompts.
1. How many times / log on to the Internet today?
2. How many text messages / send on your phone since this morning?
3. How many birthday parties / go to in the last month?
4. How many text messages / receive today?
5. How many English classes / have this week?

3 💬 Work with a partner. Ask and answer the questions in Exercise 2.

> I've only logged on to the Internet twice today. What about you?

Present perfect continuous

4 Complete the examples from the listening on page 22 then choose the correct words to complete the rules.

+	You ¹.... to classes for three weeks. We ².... once a week here in the school.
?	**Have** you **been checking** your Facebook page every day? Yes, I **have**. No, I **haven't**.

The examples above, …
1. refer to a time period that **has / hasn't** finished.
2. talk about **a single action / a series of actions**.
3. **say / don't say** how long or how regularly an action has been happening.
4. refer to actions we **expect / don't expect** to continue in the future.

➡ **Grammar reference** • page 100

5 Put the sentences in order to make a short text. How many examples of the present perfect continuous can you find?

Recently, I've been teaching myself …

a at least an hour every night. I've really been enjoying it
b on my phone and I've been practising for
c to play the guitar. I haven't been doing it for
d tutorials on YouTube! I've been watching them
e very long, just a few weeks. I've been using

… and I'm learning pretty fast!

Present perfect simple vs. present perfect continuous

6 Write sentences with the present perfect simple and the present perfect continuous.
1. I / study / English / for five years
2. I / have / two mobile phones / since I was 12
3. She / study / every evening / for the exam next week
4. He / have / three different teachers this year
5. We / take / four exams in the last month
6. I / read / a lot since September

➡ **Say it right!** • page 96

Your turn

7 Make notes about something you've been learning to do recently. Then ask and answer the questions in groups.
- How long have you been learning it?
- Why did you start?
- Who has been teaching you?
- How many times have you practised this week?
- What has been the most difficult thing to learn? Why?

23

Discover Culture

1. 💬 Work with a partner. Look at the photos and the words in the box. Describe a wedding you have been to or seen. How was it similar to the weddings in the photos?

> the clothes   the food   the music   the couple   the decorations
> the ceremony   the guests   the other members of the family

Find out about an Indian wedding.

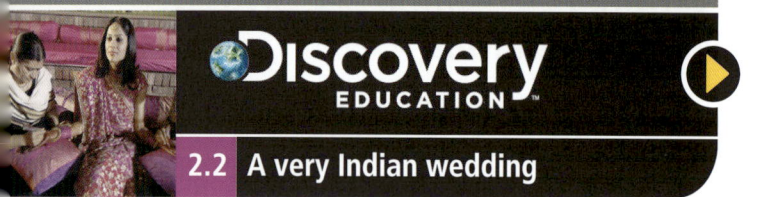

2.2 A very Indian wedding

2. ▶ 2.2 Watch the video. Which of the things in the box in Exercise 1 does it show? Was it similar to the wedding you described?

3. ▶ 2.2 Work with a partner. Are the sentences true or false? Then watch the video again and check your answers.
   1. Weddings in India aren't very big.
   2. The bride is wearing a red dress.
   3. Women paint light-coloured patterns in henna on the bride's hands.
   4. The husband dances for the bride.
   5. The rice is a sign of her love.
   6. The groom puts blue paint on the bride's hair.

4. 💬 Test your memory. Work with a partner and answer the questions.
   1. Why do they paint the bride's hands?
   2. What preparations do they make on the morning of the party?
   3. How does the groom arrive?
   4. Why does the bride give the groom rice?
   5. Why does the couple walk around the fire?

5. ▶ 2.2 Watch the video again and check your answers.

Your turn

6. Think about another traditional ceremony in your country and answer the questions with a partner.
   1. What customs do you usually see at this ceremony?
   2. What part do the various members of the family play in the ceremony?
   3. Have you ever taken part in one of these ceremonies? Did you enjoy it?

Reading A blog post

1 💬 Work with a partner. Look at the photos of a traditional Chinese wedding. What do you think is happening in each one?

2 🔊 1.26 Read the blog post. Which of the photos best fits the story? Who is telling the story? The bride? The groom? Someone else?

3 Read the blog post again. In which paragraph (1–5) can you find the following information?
  1 the food and the party   *Paragraph 5*
  2 the presents and the decorations
  3 the importance of the two families
  4 what happens on the morning of the wedding
  5 what makes a Chinese wedding different from a Western wedding
  6 why red is so important

Explore words in context

4 Match the highlighted words in the blog post with the definitions.
  1 another nice thing in addition to what you already have
  2 things you give someone on a special occasion
  3 stop doing something for a short time
  4 the time when the day starts
  5 one after the other, in order

Your turn

5 Think about the blog post. Make notes.
  • Do you think the writer enjoyed the wedding? Why/Why not?
  • Would you like to go to a Chinese wedding? Why/Why not?
  • What was the last formal party or celebration you went to? Did you enjoy it? Why/Why not?
  • How do you prefer to celebrate your birthday? With a big party or a quiet evening? Why?

6 Work with a partner. Ask and answer the questions in Exercise 5. What kind of parties do you both like? Who enjoys parties the most?

A Traditional CHINESE WEDDING

1 I'm going to **take a break** from my usual blog posts to tell you a personal story – hope you don't mind! It's a love story, with a very happy ending! It's the story of my sister's Chinese wedding.

2 For the last five years, my sister has been living and working in Beijing, and just over a year ago she and her Chinese boyfriend decided to get married. That's where the story begins!

3 In China, weddings aren't only about bringing together two people, as they are in the West, they're about bringing together two families. And in the case of my sister's wedding, two cultures. Over the past year, I've been helping her with the preparations and I've learned a lot about Chinese culture, and particularly weddings!

4 The first thing I learned was that red is a very important colour! It brings good luck, and everything to do with the wedding has to be red. The bride and groom wear red, the cars and the room where the wedding party takes place are decorated with red flowers, and the **gifts** (traditionally money) are given in small red envelopes.

5 The most important ceremonies took place on the morning of the wedding. First the groom had to come to our hotel before **sunrise**. That was really early and we'd all been up since 5 am. He asked my parents to accept him into our family and called them 'mum' and 'dad' for the first time. My parents **in turn** welcomed him into our family and called him 'son' in Chinese. He then took my sister to his home, where she was welcomed into his family. The rest of the day – the party with all the guests, the ten courses of delicious Chinese food, the music and the dancing, that's all just **a bonus**. But it was great fun!

FACT! There are more than 10 million weddings every year in China.

Speaking — Showing concern

Real talk: How have you helped a friend through a difficult situation?

1. ▶ **2.3** Watch or listen to the teenagers. What did each person do to help? Choose from the items in the box.

   > listened   lent money   made notes   doesn't say   gave advice
   > said nice things   talked   made them laugh   has never had to help

2. 💬 How have *you* helped a friend through a difficult situation? Ask and answer with your partner.

3. 🔊 **1.27** Listen to Joe and his friend Micky. What is Micky's problem?

4. Complete the conversation with the useful language.

   ### Useful language

   How can I make you feel better?
   I'm sure he'll calm down soon.
   You poor thing.
   I'm sure it will be fine.

   You don't need to worry.
   What's up?
   I know what you mean.

5. 🔊 **1.27** Listen again and check your answers.

6. 💬 Work with a partner. Practise the conversation in Exercise 4.

7. 💬 Work with a partner. Take turns to say the sentences below and respond showing concern.
   1. I've lost my new video game.
   2. I'm feeling depressed.
   3. I hate losing things.
   4. I'm worried about the exam.
   5. I've got a problem.
   6. My dad is angry with me.

8. 💬 Work with a partner. Plan your own conversation. Use the ideas below and Exercise 4 to help you.

   ### Situation 1
   Your sister took your headphones without asking and won't give them back. You think she's lost them. You've just had an argument.

   ### Situation 2
   Your parents think you are lazy. They want you to do more homework and help around the house and stop going out with your friends. You've just had an argument.

Joe: Hi Micky. ¹ *What's up?* .
Micky: Oh, I've just had another argument with my brother.
Joe: Oh! You ² .... thing. What was it about this time?
Micky: Nothing, really! He's lost a video game and he thinks I took it. But I didn't. I don't know where it is.
Joe: Well, I'm sure he'll ³ .... soon. You don't need ⁴ .... .
Micky: No, it's not that. It's just that I don't like having arguments with him.
Joe: Yes, I know ⁵ .... . I hate arguments too. But you used to be good friends.
Micky: Yes, I know. But now he gets angry all the time. I don't know what's wrong with him.
Joe: Maybe there's something worrying him. You could ask him.
Micky: Well, he has got a lot of schoolwork at the moment, before his final exams.
Joe: There you are, you see! Just be patient and I'm sure it ⁶ .... .
Micky: Yes, I suppose you're right.
Joe: Anyway, how can ⁷ .... ?
Micky: Invite me round to your house after school! That will cheer me up!

Writing A personal email

1 Read Phoebe's email. What did her grandfather give her advice about?

New mail +1

Dear Granddad,

I'm writing to thank you for your advice about my new school. I felt really lost at first! The work here is harder and the teachers seemed really strict. I found some subjects very confusing, but you were right, I just needed to explain that to the teachers. They realised I was determined to get better and since then they've been helping me a lot. Luckily, I'm hard-working!

Making friends wasn't easy. You know how shy I am, and as it's Year 3 they all knew each other already. I found it difficult to join in. Your advice to smile and ask questions worked, though. As you predicted, people smiled back! They've been happy to help me and now I've made a few friends. They've been showing me the town, and I'm feeling really happy now!

So thanks again. I don't know what I'd do without you!

Lots of love,

Phoebe xx

---

2 Read the email again and answer the questions.
1. In the first paragraph, what was Phoebe's problem and why?
2. How did she feel about it?
3. What advice did she get, and what happened?
4. In the second paragraph, why did she have a problem and what was it?
5. What advice did she get, and what happened?

Useful language

Expressing how we feel
We can use the verbs *feel* and *find* to describe our feelings.
- I *felt* really lost at first.
- I *found* some subjects very confusing.

3 Look at the Useful language box. Find two other examples of *feel* and *find* in the email.

4 Use the prompts to make sentences with *feel* or *find* which are true for you.
1. meeting new people *I find meeting new people fun.*
2. my (last) birthday
3. Maths
4. have an argument with my friends
5. a new phone
6. today

Get writing

PLAN

5 Plan an email to a friend explaining a problem. Use the questions in Exercise 2. Make notes about one of the problems below or use your own idea.

> You had a silly argument with your best friend and he/she stopped speaking to you. You don't know how to say sorry.

> You missed basketball practice because your granny was ill and then the coach didn't pick you for the team.

WRITE

6 Write your email. Use your notes from Exercise 5 and the model text to help you.

CHECK

7 Can you say YES to these questions?
- Have you explained the problem you had, the advice you got, and what happened?
- Have you included more than one paragraph?
- Have you used *feel* and *find* to describe your feelings?

1–2 Review

Vocabulary

1 Complete the descriptions of the clothes.

1 a l*eather* jacket
2 a s _ _ _ _ _ scarf 
3 f _ _ _ shoes 
4 a s _ _ _ dress 
5 a c _ _ _ hat 
6 b _ _ _ _ jeans 
7 a f _ _ _ _ _ _ skirt 
8 a f _ _ _ _ _ jacket 

2 Complete the text with the words in the box. You can use some of the words more than once.

| of | by | on | about | with |

We were really excited ¹ *about* entering the online fashion competition. I'm fascinated ² _ _ _ _ fashion design and I'm really keen ³ _ _ _ _ the latest British designers. A group of us at school created some designs especially for teenagers. We were really happy ⁴ _ _ _ _ our work and proud ⁵ _ _ _ _ our creative designs! So we were a bit disappointed ⁶ _ _ _ _ the winning entry – it wasn't original at all. Still, we aren't afraid ⁷ _ _ _ _ hard work and we're ready to try again next year.

3 Match the people (1–6) with the adjectives (a–f).

1 He's good at talking to people. *e*
2 He never gets upset or annoyed.
3 She never gives up.
4 He's quiet and not very confident.
5 He gets annoyed easily.
6 She's good at art, music and dance.

a determined
b easy-going
c impatient
d shy
e sociable
f talented

4 Choose the correct words.

LEARN A **NEW SKILL** TODAY

We've set ¹(up)/ on a new website which brings ²**about** / **together** people who want to learn skills with people who can teach them. So far, 20 people have signed ³**out** / **up**. You can offer piano lessons, for example, and in exchange, ask for someone to teach you Spanish. It's a good way for people to pass ⁴**on** / **over** their skills. Sometimes people just give ⁵**on** / **up** after one or two lessons because they don't get ⁶**in** / **on** with their teacher, but on our website, you can easily change to another teacher. Please tell all your friends about us. We're counting ⁷**over** / **on** you for your support!

Explore vocabulary

5 Choose the correct words.

1 I want to cut my hair really short and have a complete style (**change**)/ **icon**!
2 My brother works as a taxi **cab** / **driver**.
3 Have you seen the graffiti on the street **corner** / **art** over there?
4 Can I call you tonight? What's your telephone **call** / **number**?
5 I couldn't practise because one of my guitar **strings** / **bands** had broken.
6 My brother and I went to a motor **show** / **industry** last weekend.

6 Look at the underlined words in the sentences below. Are they correct? Change the form of the words when necessary.

1 You need to have a lot of determined to be an artist. *determination*
2 It's not always easy to be a successful.
3 A gymnast needs to be very flexibility.
4 It's important to be happy in your job.
5 I'm motivated by big challenging.
6 We are all passion about sports.

UNIT 1–2

Language focus

1 Choose the correct words to complete the conversation.

Joe: Granddad, where did you ¹(use)/ used to live when you were little?

Granddad: We ²wouldn't / didn't use to live in a large town. We ³used to / would live in the country. I ⁴used / would go to school by bike.

Joe: Did you ⁵use / used to wear a uniform?

Granddad: Yes, we ⁶would / did but I ⁷didn't use to / wouldn't like it very much!

Joe: ⁸Did they use to / Would they be very strict at your school in those days?

Granddad: Oh yes! They ⁹used / would get very angry if we didn't obey the rules, and we ¹⁰would / use to have to stay late at school or do extra homework.

2 Complete the text with the correct form of the past simple or past perfect. Use the verbs in brackets.

I had a terrible day yesterday! I ¹ *got* (get) home at 5 pm and I ² .... (not finish) my dinner when the phone ³ .... (ring). It was Annabel. I ⁴ .... (forget) that we ⁵ .... (arrange) to go to the cinema together! So I ⁶ .... (run) out of the house and ⁷ .... (take) a taxi to the cinema. Five minutes too late! The film ⁸ .... (start) and they ⁹ .... (not let) me in!

3 Complete the sentences with reflexive pronouns or *each other*.

1 How often do you look at *yourself* in the mirror?
2 Can we help .... to some more cake?
3 Martin taught .... to play the guitar.
4 João and Joanna talk to .... on Skype™.
5 Gabriella's parents have bought .... a new car.
6 I hurt .... when I fell over yesterday.
7 This light turns .... on when it gets dark.
8 Gabriella hurt .... when she was playing tennis.

4 Complete the conversations with the correct form of the present perfect simple or present perfect continuous. Use the verbs in brackets.

A: How many emails ¹ *have you sent* (you/send) today?
B: I ² .... (not send) many – just ten or twelve!

C: How long ³ .... (you/go) German classes?
D: About a month, but I ⁴ .... (learn) a lot already!

E: I ⁵ .... (listen) to a new band quite a lot recently – the 4tunes.
F: Really? I ⁶ .... (not hear) of them before.

Language builder

5 Choose the correct words to complete the text.

New mail +1

Hi Rob!

Guess what? I'm learning to play the piano! We ¹ *c* an old piano in our house for ages because my dad ² .... play in a rock band when he was younger. In those days, they ³ .... to have any electronic equipment like they do nowadays. Anyway, he ⁴ .... the piano for years, and I ⁵ .... about learning to play until last week when I saw a TV program about teenage musicians who have recorded ⁶ .... and put their video clips on YouTube. Some of them ⁷ .... really famous! So I've been trying to teach ⁸ .... . My dad says I ⁹ .... some progress, but my mum says the house ¹⁰ .... be a lot quieter! What's going on with you? Tell me your news! We should write to ¹¹ .... more often!

Cheers!

Lisa

	a	b	c
1	've been having	'd been having	've had
2	use to	used to	used
3	didn't use	hadn't used	didn't used
4	hadn't been touching	hadn't touch	hasn't touched
5	hadn't thought	haven't thought	don't think
6	myself	yourself	themselves
7	have become	is becoming	are become
8	each other	myself	themselves
9	's been making	've made	was making
10	use to	would	used to
11	themselves	ourselves	each other

Speaking

6 Match the sentences.

1 Do you think this T-shirt suits me?
2 You look sad. What's up?
3 Are those jeans your size?
4 I'm really upset about it.
5 Where are the changing rooms?

a I've lost my new headphones.
b No, they don't fit very well.
c Over there, on the left.
d Yes, you look great!
e You poor thing.

3 Young achievers

Discovery EDUCATION

In this unit …

- Insectmobile p33 
- The young and the brave p36 
- Saving up for something special p38 
- CLIL A cool experiment p117

Vocabulary
- Training and qualifications
- Expressions with *take*
- Achievements
- Words in context

Language focus
- *be going to* and present tenses for the future
- Predictions with *be going to*, *will* and *may/might*
- Future continuous

Unit aims
I can …
- talk about careers and training.
- understand a personal profile and a newspaper article about special young people.
- talk about future plans and make predictions about the future.
- understand a discussion on a radio news programme.
- use appropriate phrases to discuss options and make decisions.
- write an opinion essay.

BE CURIOUS

What can you see in the photo?
Start thinking
- How do you think the player is feeling?
- How old do you think he is?
- Do you know of any people who have achieved great things at a young age?

Vocabulary Training and qualifications

1 💬 Work with a partner. Look at the photos. How are they connected with learning and teaching?

2 🔊 1.28 Match words from each box to make new phrases. Then listen, check and repeat.

> university   work   application
> part-time   entrance   training   career

> experience   form   degree   path
> course   fees   exam

university degree, entrance exam, university exam …

3 Which expressions do you associate with …
a   qualifications?
b   practical training?
c   both?

4 🔊 1.29 Listen to two people talking about their plans after they leave school. Answer the questions.
1   What job do they want to do?
2   Which words or expressions from Exercise 2 do they use?

👁 Get it right!

Job refers to a specific position or profession.
My uncle's offered me a part-time ~~work~~ **job** in his café.
Work refers to the action in general.
It's ~~a~~ really interesting ~~job~~ **work**.

Your turn

5 Make notes about two people you know.
- Someone who has already finished his/her education and started work. What kind of studies did he/she do?
- Someone who has finished school but is still studying. What kind of studies is he/she doing?

6 Work with a partner. Discuss the people you know in Exercise 5. Whose studies sound most interesting? Why? What would you like to do after finishing school?

➡ **Vocabulary bank** • page 109

Reading A profile

1 💬 Work with a partner. Look at the photo of Claudette. What is she doing? How do you think she is different from other teens?

2 🔊 1.30 Read Claudette's profile and check your answers.

3 Read the profile again. Are these sentences true or false? Correct the false sentences.
1. Claudette's plan to restore the car is very recent.
2. Her parents gave her money to restore the car.
3. Her first trip in the car will be to go home.
4. She has done all the work alone.
5. Claudette plans to continue studying engineering when she leaves school.
6. Claudette hopes her story can encourage other girls to be engineers.

🔍 Explore expressions with *take*

4 Match the expressions from the profile with the synonyms below.

> take advice   take up   take place
> take time   take exams

1. have a test
2. happen
3. begin
4. do what somebody suggests
5. not to hurry

5 Complete the sentences with the correct form of the expressions in Exercise 4.
1. I always *take advice* from my teachers, they know more than me.
2. Sometimes you have to …. to make a decision so you are sure it's the right one.
3. I want to …. a job in engineering or architecture when I leave school.
4. Every year, a job fair …. in my school. You can learn a lot about different professions.
5. Everybody has to …., that's the problem with going to school!

➡ Vocabulary bank • page 109

Your turn

6 Work with a partner. What do you think of Claudette's career choice? What would be your ideal career? Why?

> I don't like Claudette's choice, because I don't like working with my hands.

HOME | ARTICLES | BLOG   sign in

MEET 13-YEAR-OLD CLAUDETTE MUÑOZ FROM ALASKA!

Claudette is a typical hard-working teenager – she studies and takes lots of exams. But there's something that makes her different. She's getting a sports car for her next birthday, but, unlike most kids her age, she's building it herself!

We spoke to Claudette about her dream car. 'Back when I was 12, I decided to restore an old car so that I could drive it on my 14th birthday. Well, I'm 13½ now, so I have six months to go … I'm going to start driving lessons as soon as I can!'

Her mum explained how she did it. 'She used the money she made working as a dog walker and bought an old Chevrolet Corvette. It's not the kind of car a teenager usually chooses but then, she isn't a typical teenager! She's worked really hard to restore it and on her 14th birthday she's going to drive that dream car to school.'

So far, Claudette has done everything herself and has fallen in love with the idea of being a mechanic. After taking advice from her teachers, her plans to train to be a mechanical engineer are now starting to come together. We asked her about the part-time training course that she's taking soon. 'My course starts next week. It takes place at a local college and lasts for three months.' But she's taking her time – it's only the first step. She wants to study for an engineering degree at the Alaska Institute for Technology. 'I know it's a strange ambition for a 13-year-old girl, but I want to be an engineer and design cars.'

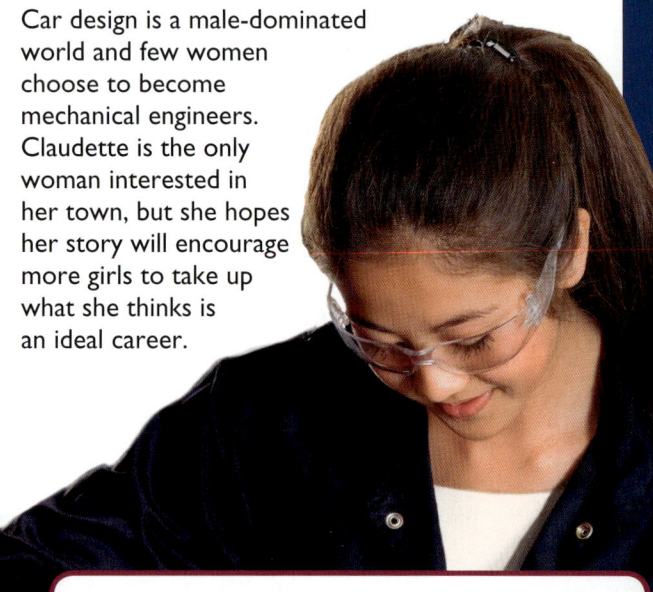

Car design is a male-dominated world and few women choose to become mechanical engineers. Claudette is the only woman interested in her town, but she hopes her story will encourage more girls to take up what she thinks is an ideal career.

FACT! *You can start to learn to drive at the age of 14 in six US states: Alaska, Arkansas, Iowa, Kansas, North Dakota and South Dakota.*

Language focus 1 *be going to* and present tenses for the future

1 Complete the examples from the text. Then complete the rules with *be going to*, present simple and present continuous.

- I**'m going to start** driving lessons as soon as I can.
- She ¹.... that dream car to school.
- I**'m starting** my holidays next week.
- She ².... a sports car for her next birthday.
- The degree course **lasts** for three years.
- My course ³.... next week.

> We use ⁴.... for future plans and intentions.
> We use ⁵.... for arrangements at a specific time in the future.
> We use ⁶.... for scheduled future events.

➜ **Grammar reference • page 101**

2 Match the beginnings and the ends of the sentences.

1. I'm very nervous because   *d*
2. I'm not feeling well, so
3. Oh, no … my exams
4. It's Sunday afternoon, so
5. The academic year
6. In the summer holidays

a starts next week.
b begin on Monday.
c I'm going to have Chinese lessons.
d I'm taking my driving test tomorrow.
e I'm not going to the party.
f I'm meeting some friends for a coffee.

3 Choose the correct form of the verbs in the text below.

Aaron Lucas is 21 and he's always dreamed of being a train driver. Today is his first day at work and Sheffield is his first destination.
The train ¹**leaves / is leaving** London St Pancras at 2.30 and ²**is arriving / arrives** two hours later. Next week, he ³**'s going to drive / drives** trains further – to Newcastle, Edinburgh and Aberdeen.
And the good news is that he ⁴**doesn't travel / isn't travelling** alone, the whole family ⁵**take / are taking** the train with him on his first day. He ⁶**'s going to work / works** all week, but for them it's a holiday!

4 Complete the sentences with the correct future form of the verbs in brackets.

1. My holidays .... (start) soon, hooray!
2. My class .... (finish) at 6 pm, but I have to stay late.
3. I .... (not study) anymore when I'm 18, I want to start work.
4. I .... (see) the dentist tomorrow at 4 pm, I'm scared!
5. I .... (not meet) anybody after school this week, I have to study ☹!
6. I .... (learn) Chinese, it's the language of the future.

5 Which of the sentences in Exercise 4 are plans? Are any of the plans true for you? Change them so that they are true.

I'm meeting my friend Antonio after school on Thursday. We're …

Your turn

6 Make notes about five plans you have for the next week.

7 Swap your plans with a partner. Then ask for more information about each plan.

> What are your plans for next week?

> On Saturday, I'm meeting my friends …

Learn about the insectmobile.
- Can you imagine a vehicle that has legs not wheels?
- What would it look like?
- What insect would it look like?

Discovery EDUCATION
3.1 Insectmobile

Listening A discussion

1 💬 **Work with a partner. Look at the photos and answer the questions.**
1. What can you see in the photos?
2. What do you think is the connection between the girl and the flip-flops?
3. What's special about her flip-flops?

2 🔊 1.31 **Listen to a discussion on a radio news programme and check your answers.**

3 🔊 1.31 **Read this short profile of Madison Nicole Robinson, better known as Madison Nicole. Then listen again and find five more mistakes.**

> FishFlops® are an amazing new fashion. Teenager Madison Nicole had the idea for FishFlops® at the age of ~~13~~ 8 and started her business immediately. She developed the whole project herself and sold 70,000 pairs in her first year. The FishFlops® sold for £25 a pair. This is how she became a millionaire. But she's not greedy, she also helps charities. For example, she gave away 15,000 pairs of FishFlops® to people in need. She also does other voluntary work to support the community. Sometimes, she signs them and donates them as well.

Vocabulary Achievements

4 🔊 1.32 **Look at the expressions from the radio programme. Which ones are about a) money, b) fame, c) work and d) helping others? Then listen, check and repeat.**
1. She **started a business** when she was 13.
2. She's **made a fortune**, 60,000 pairs at $25 a pair!
3. She's **become a millionaire**.
4. She'll be **winning awards** for her business idea.
5. She's **developed the project** herself.
6. She **does voluntary work** in the community.
7. I bet she's going to **break records**, too …
8. It's great to **support the community**.

5 Complete the sentences with the correct form of expressions from Exercise 4.
1. I don't want to _become a millionaire_, I'm not interested in money.
2. I'd like to …. locally, you don't need to travel to help others in need.
3. It's hard to …. if you don't have any original ideas.
4. My neighbour …. selling T-shirts she made in her garage – £20,000!
5. She …. for that design, it was a well-deserved prize.
6. I don't want to …. myself, it's too much responsibility.

Your turn

6 Look at the achievements in Exercise 4 and put them in order of importance for you. Discuss your ideas with a partner.

> I think that winning awards is the most important thing for me.

> Really? I don't agree. I think …

➡ **Vocabulary bank** • page 109

34

Language focus 2 Predictions with *be going to*, *will* and *may/might*

1 Complete the examples from the listening on page 34. Then match the beginnings and the ends of the sentences to complete the rules.

> 'll win   's going to be   will be   might become

1 It's on the front page of all the local papers, it .... today's top story.
2 She .... the richest teenager in the States, I don't know.
3 Yes, she should, I'm sure she .... !
4 Meanwhile, her FishFlops® .... the latest fashion.

1 We use *be going to*	a to show that we are not sure about a prediction.
2 We use *will*	b to make a general prediction, or to give an opinion about the future.
3 We use *may* or *might*	c to make a prediction based on evidence.

➜ **Grammar reference** • page 101

2 Look at the pictures. What is going to happen? Use the verbs in the box to make predictions.

> rain   fall over   slip   score

1 *I think the bricks are going to …*

3 Choose the correct form of the verbs in the sentences below.

1 I hope I **'ll make / might make** a fortune when I'm older.
2 **A:** Look! She **'ll win / 's going to win** the race.
   B: Well … She **might win / won't win**, but I'm not sure.
3 He doesn't look very well, it looks like he **'ll faint / 's going to faint**.
4 **A:** Look at the blue sky! It **'ll be / 's going to be** a lovely day.
   B: You never know, the weather **is going to change / may change** quickly.
5 All my friends **will / may** be at the party tonight I expect. Only Ben can't come.

Future continuous

4 Complete the examples from the listening on page 34. Then choose the correct words to complete the rules.

+	Everybody ¹.... them on the beach this summer. She ².... awards for her business idea.
−	He **won't be doing** much voluntary work this year, he's too busy.
?	So, **will** you **be buying** a pair of FishFlops®, Glenda? Yes I **will**. No, I **won't**.

- We use the future continuous to **make predictions about the future / give opinions**.
- We **use / don't use** the future continuous with state verbs.

➜ **Grammar reference** • page 101

5 🔊 **1.33** Put the underlined words in order to complete the text. Then listen and check.

By 2050,
… experts think that ¹doing / be / will / we everything via our smartphones. They say that ²speaking / we / be / will with operating systems all the time, so ³alone / won't / we / be!
… ⁴learning / be / won't / we English anymore, because ⁵know / everybody / it / will.
… ⁶have / won't / we cars that use petrol, ⁷be / will / driving / we greener vehicles.
… ⁸longer / we / living / be / will, because ⁹discovering / doctors / be / will new medicines all the time.
… ¹⁰won't / life / be / better but it will be very different!

➜ **Say it right!** • page 96

Your turn

6 Work with a partner. Look at the predictions in Exercise 5. Which are positive and which negative? Which do you agree with?

7 Think about your own life in the next 30 years. What will you be doing? Compare your ideas with a partner.

> I think I'll be working in a bank …

Discover Culture

1. 💬 **Work with a partner. Look at the photos and answer the questions.**
   1. What's the difference between the two horse races?
   2. Where do you think the two photos were taken? Why?
   3. What is special about the race at the bottom do you think?

   Find out about the Naadam festival horse race.

   3.2 The young and the brave

2. ▶ 3.2 **Watch the video without sound. Put the images you see in order.**
   a. horse riders doing tricks
   b. children with horses in a field
   c. horse riders with flags
   d. children racing on horses
   e. skyscrapers

3. ▶ 3.2 **Watch the video with sound. Are the sentences about conventional horse races or the Naadam festival horse race?**
   1. horse riders are usually adults
   2. horse riders can be as young as five years old
   3. races last about 2 kilometres
   4. races last 30 kilometres
   5. they ride with saddles
   6. they ride without saddles

4. ▶ 3.2 **Complete the text with the words in the box. One word is repeated. Then watch the video from 02.02 to 02.28 and check your answers.**

   > courage   balance   strength

   They'll need incredible [1].... and [2].... to stay on their horses. When their horses get tired, the children sing to them. Who is the winner of this year's race going to be? We don't know yet. But it is the children's [3].... and [4].... that make them all winners.

   Your turn

5. **Ask and answer with your partner.**
   1. What most surprised you about the video?
   2. What images have stayed in your mind?
   3. What else would you like to know about the Naadam festival?

   > It surprised me that the winner was not important ...

6. **Have you or has someone you know competed in a race? What was the sport? What skills/qualities did they need to do the sport?**

Inner Mongolia
China

YOUNG AUSTRALIAN OF THE YEAR AWARD

UNIT 3

Australia

Do you know somebody who has done something special? Should they win a prize for it? Well, if you're Australian, every year you can recommend a **fellow** Australian for an award. The Young Australian of the Year Award is for young people between the ages of 16 and 30, and for personal, academic or professional achievements. There are so many recommendations, it's **virtually** impossible to know who will win, so the vote is very exciting. Each of the 8 states selects 4 people, so the winner is chosen from a **shortlist** of 32.

One winner, Akram Azimi, worked with Aboriginal communities in **remote** Western Australia. This is amazing because he arrived in Australia as a **refugee** from Afghanistan when he was just 13, so English is not his first language. Akram used his natural skills as a leader to help young people work and study in rural communities.

Other winners include the swimmer Ian Thorpe. Like many sportspeople, Thorpe started very young. At the age of 14, he became the youngest male ever to represent Australia and his victory in the 1998 Perth World Championships made him the youngest ever individual male World Champion. Thorpe won the Young Australian of the Year award after breaking records and winning gold medals at the Sydney Olympics.

Meanwhile, other prizes have gone to people of great bravery. Trisha Broadbridge became famous in Australia for surviving the 2004 tsunami in Thailand. Her husband sadly died in the tragedy. She set up the Broadbridge Fund, a charity which helped to build the Broadbridge Education Centre on Thailand's Phi Phi island.

The award is announced on the eve of Australia Day (26th January) and is very popular with Australian people. On the night of the 25th, the nation will be watching to find out this year's winner!

FACT! The 2014 award was given to swimmer Jacqueline Freney, who was born with cerebral palsy. She won eight gold medals at the London Paralympic Games.

Reading A newspaper article

1 💬 Work with a partner. Look at the photos and answer the questions.
   1 What do you think these people have in common?
   2 What do you think they have achieved?
   3 Which person do you think is famous for doing sport? Why? What sport do you think he/she is famous for?

2 🔊 1.36 Read the newspaper article and check your answers.

3 Read the article again and answer the questions.
   1 Why is it difficult to predict the winner of the award?
   2 How many finalists are there each year?
   3 Why is Akram Azimi's achievement so great?
   4 What did Ian Thorpe achieve at 14?
   5 Who was able to do something good after a bad experience?
   6 Why is the date of the awards ceremony so special?

Explore words in context

4 Match the highlighted words in the article with the definitions.
   1 a small number of candidates for something
   2 almost
   3 far away
   4 someone who has been forced to leave their country
   5 someone who is in the same situation as you

Your turn

5 Think of somebody in your country who deserves a prize. Who is it? What have they achieved? Make notes.

6 Work with a partner and discuss your ideas. Whose is the biggest achievement? Why?

> My cousin won a national athletics competition when he was fifteen!

Speaking Making decisions

Real talk: Are you saving up for something special? What?

1. ▶ **3.3** Watch or listen to the teenagers. Complete the sentences with what each person is saving up for.
   1. Concert .... for her .....
   2. A(n) .... guitar.
   3. A second-hand .... if his parents agree.
   4. Saving up for .... in two years, and travel.
   5. A(n) .... with his friend's family.

2. 💬 Are *you* saving up for something special? What? Ask and answer with your partner.

3. 🔊 **1.37** Listen to Bella and Joseph discussing giving money to a charity. What do they decide to do?

4. Complete the conversation with the useful language.

   ### Useful language
   How shall we decide, then?
   I was thinking of …
   We need to decide …
   Personally, I'd rather …
   I think the best way is …
   That's a good idea, too.
   What kind of thing do you suggest?

Bella:	Joseph! We have to make a decision about the class cake sale next month.
Joseph:	Mmm. ¹ *We need to decide* who to give the money to, right?
Bella:	Yes! I was ² .... Oxfam or UNICEF. What do you think?
Joseph:	I think a local charity would be better.
Bella:	Right. How about the animal sanctuary? I know someone who works there.
Joseph:	Personally, ³ .... support an organisation that helps young people.
Bella:	OK! ⁴ .... do you suggest?
Joseph:	Well, my sister is a volunteer at a disabled teenagers club. They organise social activities and weekend trips.
Bella:	Yes, that's ⁵ .... , too.
Joseph:	My sister says they're always looking for donations.
Bella:	So is the animal sanctuary. They help animals whose owners didn't look after them.
Joseph:	Mmm. That's a good cause, too. How ⁶ .... , then?
Bella:	I think ⁷ .... to vote in class.
Joseph:	Yes, I agree. Let's do it tomorrow.

5. 🔊 **1.37** Listen again and check your answers.

6. 💬 Work with a partner. Practise the conversation in Exercise 4.

7. Which of the phrases in Exercise 4 is …
   a. giving an opinion?
   b. suggesting something?
   c. asking for the other person's opinion?

8. 💬 Work with a partner. Plan your own conversation. Use the ideas below and Exercise 4 to help you.

   Decision to be made: How to raise money for the class end-of-year trip.
   Possibilities: a sponsored cycle ride; selling lottery/raffle tickets with a prize; selling food at school break time; a collection in the town square.

Writing — An opinion essay

1 Look at the title and read the essay. Does the writer agree or disagree?

The school leaving age should be 18. Do you agree?

Whereas my grandparents left school at 14, nowadays the minimum age in many countries is 16, and increasingly, 18. However, I believe it might not be the best idea to make everyone stay at school until they are 18.

Firstly, although those students who want to go to university will stay at school until they are 18, not everyone enjoys studying. There are other options for people that aren't going to go to university, and many young people would rather look for work, do a training course or get work experience where they can learn practical skills which will help them to find a job.

In addition, there is the problem that some over-16s who don't want to stay on at school will behave badly, and as a result will create problems for everyone else in their class.

In conclusion I'm against it, at least until schools can provide a wider range of training courses and work experience.

2 Read the essay again and identify which paragraph each of these points is in.
   a   an argument in favour of your opinion
   b   the situation now and in the past
   c   a personal opinion (two paragraphs)
   d   a summary of the arguments
   e   another argument to support your opinion

Useful language

Linking phrases
We use linking words and phrases to show contrast:
Whereas my grandparents left school at …
or to show the order of arguments:
Firstly, although those students who …

3 Look at the Useful language box. Find two other words that show contrast and two other phrases that show the order of arguments in the essay.

4 Complete the sentences with the phrases in the box.

> however   firstly   in conclusion   in addition   whereas   although

   1   You could work as a waiter, …. there are other options.
   2   …. getting a part-time job is a good idea, students may not be able to study enough.
   3   Learning how to cook is common, …. learning car mechanics isn't.
   4   …., I agree that learning practical skills at school is useful, and …. to this, it's fun!
   5   …. I agree with all pupils doing work experience.

Get writing

PLAN

5 Plan an essay for one of the titles below. Use Exercise 2 to help you decide what to put in each paragraph.

> All pupils should be taught practical skills at school, like cooking or driving.

> All school leavers should do three months work experience.

WRITE

6 Write your essay. Use your notes from Exercise 5 and the model text to help you.

CHECK

7 Can you say YES to these questions?
   • Have you included all the essential information from Exercise 2?
   • Have you used linking words and phrases to show contrast and show the order of arguments?

4 Fabulous food

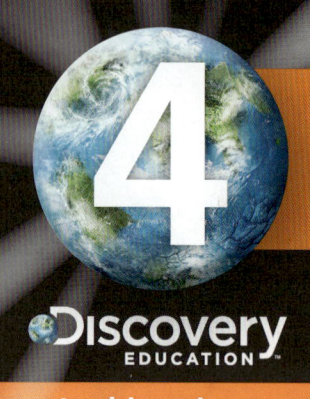

Discovery EDUCATION

In this unit ...

- Oil from goats? **p43** 
- Fruits of the sea **p46** 
- Cooking for your family **p48** 
- CLIL You are what you eat **p118**

Vocabulary
- Cooking verbs
- Words in context
- Adjectives describing food
- Prepositional phrases

Language focus
- First conditional with *if*, *when* and *unless*
- Second conditional with *could* and *might*

Unit aims
I can ...
- talk about how to prepare simple dishes.
- understand short online texts and an online article about different foods.
- discuss possible and imaginary situations in the present and future.
- understand a game show where people describe food.
- give instructions on how to make a dish.
- describe a local dish.

BE CURIOUS

What can you see in the photo?
Start thinking
- What does the picture show and what is it made of?
- Would you like to eat it? Why/Why not?
- Have you ever made any food art?

Vocabulary Cooking verbs

1 🔊 1.38 Match the verbs in the box with the photos (a–j). Then listen, check and repeat.

> roast   mix   chop   slice   bake   boil   grill   fry   grate   spread

2 Match the foods in the box with the verbs in Exercise 1 to make instructions.

> eggs   bread   cake   cheese   pasta
> chicken   steak   onion   garlic
> tomatoes   sauce   butter

fry eggs, boil eggs, fry chicken …

3 🔊 1.39 Listen to someone explaining how to make a dish. Copy and complete the table below. Would you like to try it? Why/Why not?

ingredients	cooking verbs

Your turn

4 Ask and answer with your partner.
1. Do you ever do any cooking?
2. What can you cook?
3. What was the last thing you cooked?

5 Choose a simple recipe you know. Explain how to cook it to your partner.

> I can make cheese on toast! First, you grate some cheese …

➡ **Vocabulary bank** • page 110

DANGEROUS FOODS?

Everyone knows that chopping onions can make you cry. It's because onions release a **toxic** gas when you cut them or fry them. When the gas gets into your eyes, your body produces tears to wash it out. So, next time you chop an onion, do it under a running tap. If you cut the onion under running water, the gas won't get into your eyes!

Did you know that peanuts are poisonous for dogs and can be very dangerous for humans too if you are allergic to them? Even the smallest piece of peanut can cause a very bad reaction. If one day you have an **allergic** reaction to a peanut, you will need to get to a hospital as quickly as you can!

The 'fugu' is the world's most poisonous fish – and it's also one of the most expensive! It's a **delicacy** in Japan, but eating the tiniest drop of the toxins in its **intestines** can kill you! Specially trained fugu chefs learn how to slice the fish very carefully to avoid any contamination. If you are ever in Japan and want to try fugu fish for yourself, you'll have to be very careful! You'll need to make sure you go to a restaurant that has a 'fugu certified' chef unless you want it to be your last supper!

FACT! In the Second World War, doctors used the water in green coconuts to replace blood plasma.

Reading Short online texts

1 💬 Work with a partner. Look at the photos. What kind of food can you see in each image? How dangerous do you think they could be? Why?

2 🔊 1.40 Read the webpage. Order the food from the least dangerous to the most dangerous.

3 Read the webpage again. Copy and complete the table.

Food	Possible dangers	Advice
onions	They can make you ^{1}…. when you chop them.	Chop them under ^{2}….
peanuts	They are poisonous for ^{3}…. and they can cause a bad ^{4}…. in some humans.	Get to a(n) ^{5}…. as soon as you can.
fugu fish	They are extremely ^{6}….	Only eat fugu fish that has been prepared by a(n) ^{7}….
garlic	It can give you a serious ^{8}….	Don't let it get in contact with your ^{9}….

Explore words in context

4 Match the highlighted words in the webpage with the definitions.
1 long tubes that take food from your stomach
2 a food which people think is very special
3 having an extreme reaction to specific types of food
4 poisonous
5 serious

Your turn

5 Ask and answer with your partner.
1 Are you going to change any of your eating habits after reading the article?
2 Would you try fugu fish? Why/Why not?
3 Do you know about any other foods that can be dangerous?

Garlic has a lot of positive qualities. Throughout history people have believed that it has powerful medicinal uses. It can also protect you from mosquito bites. I always get mosquito bites in summer, so when I go on holiday this year, I'll make sure I eat lots of garlic! But don't put fresh garlic on the bites! Fresh garlic is very strong and a slice of garlic can give you a **severe** burn if it is in contact with your skin!

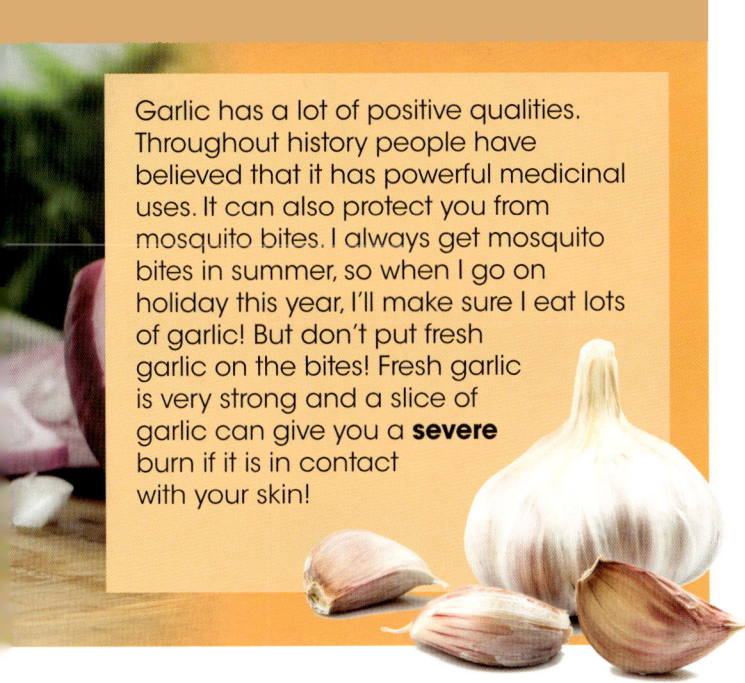

Language focus 1 First conditional with *if, when* and *unless*

1 Complete the examples from the text. Then match the missing words with the meanings (a–c).

1 …. you are ever in Japan and want to try fugu fish for yourself, you'll have to be very careful!
2 You'll need to make sure you go to a restaurant that has a 'fugu certified' chef …. you want it to be your last supper!
3 …. I go on holiday this year, I'll make sure I eat lots of garlic!

a This introduces a situation in the future that you are sure is going to happen.
b This introduces a situation that is possible in the future, but you're not sure it's going to happen.
c This introduces a situation in the future that means the consequence won't happen.

➡ Grammar reference • page 102

2 Match the beginnings and the ends of the sentences.

1 When she finishes her exams,
2 If he fails the exam,
3 My mum won't let me go out
4 Unless you hurry up,
5 I'll call you this evening
6 If I get home before 10 pm,

a he may be really disappointed.
b when I get home.
c she'll be so happy!
d I might call you.
e unless I finish my homework.
f we'll miss the bus!

Get it right!

Don't use *will* after *if, when* or *unless*.
If you will eat too many carrots, your skin will turn a light orange colour! ✗

3 🔊 1.41 Complete the conversation using *if, when* and *unless* or the correct form of the verbs in brackets. Then listen and check.

Julia: Hi Marie! How's the food going? Do you need any help?
Marie: Yes, please! ¹…. you ²…. (finish) preparing these sandwiches, I ³…. (put) the drinks on the table.
Julia: Anything else?
Marie: Yes, ⁴…. the guests arrive, they'll need to put their coats somewhere. Do you think you can do that for me?
Julia: Yes, sure. We ⁵…. (put) them in your room, on the bed, ⁶…. you want me to put them somewhere else?
Marie: No, on the bed is great! Oh … and ⁷…. I get my CD player, ⁸…. (you/choose) some CDs and put some music on in the living room?
Julia: Of course! A great party needs great music!

Your turn

4 Organise a special dinner for your friends. Use sentences with *if, when* and *unless*. Decide who will …

- do the shopping.
- prepare the food.
- prepare the decorations.

If you make the starters, I'll prepare the main course.

When the starters are ready, I'll …

I'll … , unless you want to do it!

Learn about Argan oil.
- What can you see in the tree?
- Why do you think it is there?
- What kind of food can you get from a goat?

4.1 Oil from goats?

Vocabulary Adjectives describing food

1 🔊 1.42 Match the adjectives in bold with the definitions (a–j). Then listen, check and repeat.

1. I can't eat this soup, it's too **salty**!
2. Mmm, these strawberries are **delicious**! I love them!
3. Quick, give me some water, this sauce is really **spicy**! My tongue's on fire!
4. I'm sorry, but I can't eat this. It's totally **disgusting**!
5. Mmm … did you forget to put salt on the pasta? It tastes very **bland**.
6. Wow, this cake is very **sweet**!
7. I don't like fried mushrooms, they're too **slimy**.
8. Yuk, this coffee hasn't got any sugar in it! It's really **bitter**!
9. Have you tried these apples? They're great, so **crunchy**!
10. I don't really like chocolate or cakes, I prefer **savoury** snacks like nuts and crisps.

a It has a lot of sugar in it.   *sweet*
b It has a lot of salt in it.
c It tastes hot in your mouth.
d It doesn't taste good.
e It tastes very good.
f It doesn't taste of anything in particular.
g It's hard and makes a noise when you eat it.
h It's soft and oily and not very nice!
i It's salty and not made with sugar.
j It's unpleasant and not sweet.

➡ Vocabulary bank • page 110

2 Which adjectives in Exercise 1 describe a) taste, b) texture (how they feel in your mouth) and c) a good or bad opinion?

taste – salty …

Listening A game show

3 💬 Work with a partner. Look at the photos. Use adjectives from Exercise 1 to describe each dish.

4 🔊 1.43 Listen to a competition where people taste the three mystery dishes in the photos. Which dish is the most popular?

5 🔊 1.43 Listen again and copy and complete the notes for each dish.

Main ingredients	Country of origin	Adjectives used to describe the dish
1 ᵃ jellyfish / onions	ᵇ China / Japan / Vietnam	ᶜ ….
2 ᵈ ears / cockscombs	ᵉ France / Italy / Spain	ᶠ ….
3 ᵍ chilli peppers / grasshoppers	ʰ Colombia / Korea / Mexico	ⁱ ….

Your turn

6 Ask and answer with your partner.
1. Would you like to try these dishes? Why/Why not?
2. Have you ever eaten an unusual dish or seen someone else eating something strange? What was it? Did it taste good?
3. Do you like trying new foods? Why/Why not?
4. What's your favourite dish? What does it taste like?

Language focus 2 Second conditional with *could* and *might*

1 Match the beginnings and the ends of the sentences from the listening on page 44.

1 If I saw it on a menu,   a if you had the chance?
2 I wouldn't eat it again   b I might eat it again.
3 Would you eat it again   c if you offered it to me.
4 I could eat that again   d if you paid me!

2 Look at the examples in Exercise 1 and complete the rules with the words and phrases in the box. There are three that you don't need to use.

> could   present simple   at the end   might
> in the middle   would   past simple   will

1 To form the second conditional, use *if* + ... for the situation, and *would*, ... or .... for a possible consequence.
2 To form questions, use (question word) + ... + subject + verb, e.g.
What would you do if someone offered you a slice of fried snake?
3 *If* can come at the beginning or .... of the sentence/question, e.g.
If I paid you, would you try it?
Would you try it if I paid you?

> Use the second conditional to talk about situations that are **real / imaginary**.

➡ Grammar reference • page 102

3 Choose the correct form of the verbs in the sentences below.
1 I **never ate / could never eat** snake unless I **was / 'd be** very hungry!
2 **You would like / Would you like** to taste jellyfish salad if you **got / 'd get** the chance?
3 If I **had / 'd have** to choose between giving up chocolate or pizza, I **gave up / 'd give up** chocolate!
4 If I **was / 'd be** a fugu chef, I **was / might be** a little worried about poisoning my customers!
5 Unless I **picked / 'd pick** them myself, I **never ate / 'd never eat** wild mushrooms. They could be poisonous!
6 If someone **offered / would offer** you food you **didn't like / wouldn't like**, what **you would say / would you say**?

4 Write second conditional questions using the prompts.
1 What / do / if / forget / your mum's birthday? *What would you do if you forgot your mum's birthday?*
2 What / say / if / a friend ask / you to lend her some money?
3 If / you can live / anywhere in the world / where / like / to live?
4 If / you win / the lottery / what / do / with the money?
5 What advice / you give / your friend / if he / be worried about his exams?
6 If / you not need / to study this evening / what / do instead?

➡ Say it right! • page 96

5 💬 Work with a partner. Ask and answer the questions in Exercise 4. Add two more questions using your own ideas.

Your turn

6 Work with a partner. Write two lists of food.
- Food I would never eat no matter what!
- Food I would eat in order to survive on a desert island.

7 Work with another pair. Compare your answers then choose the five most disgusting foods you know of and the five most delicious.

> I could never eat jellyfish. It sounds disgusting!

> Me neither – yuk! And what about grasshoppers?

Discover Culture

1 💬 Work with a partner. What do you know about Japan? Think about the topics in the box.

| geography | food | people | work | entertainment | cities | sport |

Find out about fishing in Japan.

4.2 Fruits of the sea

2 ▶ 4.2 Watch the video. Which of the topics in Exercise 1 does it talk about?

3 ▶ 4.2 Watch the video again and choose the best summary.
1. People in Japan live a long time because they eat so much fish.
2. The sea plays a very important role in the lives and diet of the Japanese people.
3. The Japanese eat more fish than any other nation in the world.

4 Test your memory. Which images below did you see in the video? Think of three more images you remember from the video.
- the islands and seas surrounding Japan
- modern skyscrapers and cities
- traffic in the busy cities
- young people having fun
- old people being active
- fishing boats
- tuna, squid and shellfish
- fresh fish in a restaurant

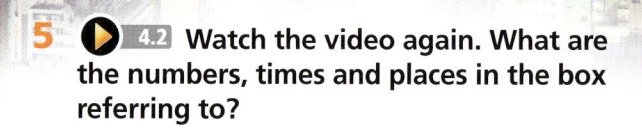

5 ▶ 4.2 Watch the video again. What are the numbers, times and places in the box referring to?

| 10%   over 80   at night
| deep water of northern Japan   over 40,000
| restaurants and supermarkets |

6 ▶ 4.2 Work with a partner. Match the fish to the facts. Then watch the video from 01.12 to 02.02 and check your answers.

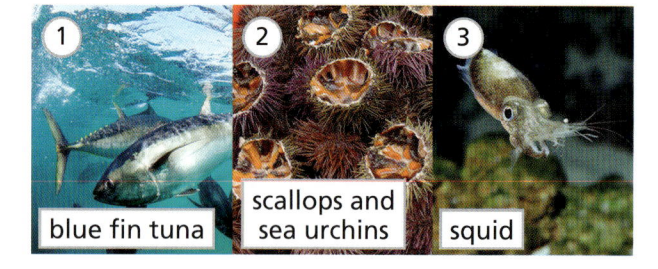

1. blue fin tuna
2. scallops and sea urchins
3. squid

a It's one of the most popular fish in Japan.
b It's full of protein and vitamins.
c They live close to the shore.
d They live further out in deeper water.
e They like the lights on the boats.

Your turn

7 Think about the video. Did you learn anything new about Japan?

8 Ask and answer with your partner.
1. Is fish or seafood an important part of your diet? Why/Why not?
2. What is the most popular food in your country? Do you like it? Why/Why not?

Reading An online article

1 Work with a partner. Look at the photos. What kind of food can you see? Where do you think the foods come from?

2 **1.46** Read the online article about food from different countries and check your answers.

3 Read the article again and identify the countries.
   1 The most common food in this country is meat. *Mongolia*
   2 This country has no coast.
   3 They eat rice cooked in a special way in this country.
   4 They cook food on hot rocks in this country.
   5 This country has a lot of volcanoes.

Explore prepositional phrases

4 Choose the correct words. Then check your answers in the article.
   1 A country surrounded **by / for** land, like Mongolia, depends on meat.
   2 It is eaten **in / on** a number of different ways.
   3 With our busy modern lifestyles where everyone is always **in / on** the go, street food is the obvious answer.
   4 From Turkish sımıt bread sellers **in / on** the streets of Istanbul to Thai noodle carts in Bangkok.

5 Complete the questions with the prepositions and underlined phrases in Exercise 4.
   1 What do busy people in cities eat when they are ....?
   2 Is your country surrounded by sea or ....?
   3 What is the most important ingredient in your country's food? Can you prepare it ....?
   4 In your town, is there food for sale ....?

→ Vocabulary bank • page 110

Your turn

6 Work with a partner. Ask and answer the questions in Exercise 5.

7 Discuss the questions.
   1 What are the main influences on food in your country?
   2 Is traditional food popular in your country or do people prefer food from other countries?
   3 Where and when do you usually eat street food? What kind do you prefer? Why?

> The main ingredients are typical Mediterranean ingredients …

WHAT INFLUENCES THE FOOD ON YOUR PLATE?

The food we eat is influenced by so many things: our geography, our history, our climate and our lifestyle. So just as a country surrounded by sea, like Japan, is a nation of fish-eaters, a country surrounded by land, like Mongolia (where the nearest coast is 700 kilometres away), depends on meat. Mutton, the meat from sheep, is the most important ingredient in Mongolian food. It is eaten in a number of different ways, roasted, in soup or the most popular of all, in dumplings called buuz.

But it isn't only the ingredients that change, ways of preparing food can depend on geography too. In New Zealand, a land with more than 60 volcanoes, the Maori use a method called hāngi to prepare food. They use volcanic rock to cook the food underground. They dig a large hole where they make a fire to heat the rocks. The food goes on the rocks, they close the hole and wait for four or five hours for the food to cook. If you walked by a cooking hāngi, you wouldn't even know it was there! You can't even smell the food cooking.

But we can't always wait five hours for our food. With our busy modern lifestyles where everyone is always on the go, street food is the obvious answer and each country has its traditional street food, from Turkish sımıt bread sellers on the streets of Istanbul to Thai noodle carts in Bangkok. In Sicily, in southern Italy, traditional street food is a ball of fried rice called an arancino. The centre of the ball is filled with a rich tomato and meat sauce. It is just as delicious as a bowl of pasta or a slice of pizza, but so much easier to eat as you walk down the street. If I had to choose my favourite fast food, this would be it!

WHAT ABOUT YOUR COUNTRY?
What influences the kind of food people eat where you live?

FACT! 2.5 billion people around the world eat street food every day.

Speaking Giving instructions

Real talk: What would you make if you had to cook for your family for a day?

1 🎬 **4.3** Watch or listen to the teenagers. What food items does each person talk about?

> omelette   sandwiches   salad   vegetables   eggs   rice dish   soup   cake   chicken
> steak   pizzas   berry pie   potato salad   lasagne   pancakes   meat   pasta

2 💬 What would *you* make if you had to cook for your family for a day? Ask and answer with your partner.

3 🔊 **1.47** Listen to Josh talking to his mum on the phone. What is he going to make?

a spaghetti bolognese

b soup

c an omelette

4 Complete the conversation with the useful language.

Useful language

You need to stir it …   Next, you …
Finally, when …   The first thing to do is …
First of all, chop …   Then, add …

Mum: Right, Josh. ¹ *The first thing to do is* get out the ingredients. You'll need an onion, two cloves of garlic, a tin of chopped tomatoes, the packet of mince from the fridge and some tomato puree.

Josh: OK, I'll write down what I have to do.

Mum: Ready? ² …. the onion and the garlic and fry them gently with some oil until they're soft. ³ …. add the mince to the pan. ⁴ …. for a few minutes until it's brown.

Josh: OK. It sounds simple enough. What else?

Mum: ⁵ …. the tin of tomatoes, a tablespoon of tomato puree, some water to cover the meat, and salt and pepper.

Josh: OK. Then what?

Mum: ⁶ …. it boils, turn the heat down low. And that's it! If you put a lid on it and let it cook gently, it will be ready when I get home.

5 🔊 **1.47** Listen again and check your answers.

6 💬 Work with a partner. Practise the conversation in Exercise 4.

7 💬 Work with a partner. Plan your own conversation. Use the ideas below and Exercise 4 to help you.

> **Dish:** Cheesy pasta bake 
>
> **Ingredients:** 140g pasta, 2 onions, 2 carrots, 4 cloves of garlic, tomatoes, grated cheese
>
> **Cooking instructions:** slice onion and garlic, fry gently; add chopped vegetables; boil pasta for 12 minutes; mix everything in a dish; bake for 20 minutes; serve with cheese on top.

> **Dish:** Vegetable and cheese omelette 
>
> **Ingredients:** 4 eggs, 1 onion, mushrooms, red pepper, grated cheese, 20g butter
>
> **Cooking instructions:** chop vegetables, fry in butter until soft; mix vegetables and eggs together; put in pan and fry for 2 minutes; add grated cheese on top and cook for 2–3 minutes more.

Writing Describing a local dish

1 Look at the photo and read the description on an Internet forum. What is the dish Lamorna describes and what is it made from?

I live in Cornwall, in south-west England, and we have lots of delicious local food, but our most famous dish is the Cornish pasty! A traditional pasty consists of thick pastry in a D-shape, filled with small pieces of steak, potato, onion and an orange vegetable called swede. Then it's baked in the oven.

Pasties are usually served hot, on their own, and are easy to eat without a knife and fork. Many years ago, Cornish workers used to eat pasties for lunch. Nowadays, tourists eat them on the beach!

You can eat pasties all over Britain, but unless they are made in Cornwall, they can't be called Cornish pasties. Local pasty shops sell pasties with many different fillings, like curried chicken or cheese and onion. So if you want to try a real Cornish pasty, get down to Cornwall!

Lamorna

2 Read the description again. In which paragraph does Lamorna talk about these things? Which two things in the list doesn't she mention?

The ingredients.
Where the food is from.
Who eats it.
Why people like it.
Where you can buy it.
The history of the dish.
How it's cooked.
When you eat it.
How easy or difficult it is to cook.

Useful language

Cooking and eating

When we write about food, we use phrases to describe the ingredients and how it's cooked and eaten.
- *A traditional pasty **consists of** …*
- *It **contains** vegetables and meat.*
- *It's **served with** salad.*
- *They're **fried in** olive oil.*

3 Look at the Useful language box. Find similar phrases in the text.

4 Complete the sentences with the phrases in the box.

> bake in   filled with   consists of   made in   contain   served with

1 A traditional Sunday lunch is .... vegetables and roast potatoes.
2 Mix all the ingredients together and then .... the cake .... the oven for half an hour.
3 Ravioli are pasta squares .... meat or cheese.
4 It's a simple dish which .... rice and vegetables.
5 Only cheese that is actually .... Cheddar can be called Cheddar cheese.
6 I don't eat many sweets – they .... too much sugar.

Get writing

PLAN

5 Choose a local or traditional dish to write about. Use the list in Exercise 2 and make notes.

WRITE

6 Write your description for the Internet forum. Use your notes from Exercise 5 and the model text to help you.

CHECK

7 Can you say YES to these questions?
- Have you included all the important information from Exercise 2?
- Have you used phrases to describe different aspects of the dish?

UNIT 4

49

3–4 Review

Vocabulary

1 Complete the sentences with the words in the box.

> fees   course   experience
> ~~degree~~   form   exam   job

1 I have a university _degree_ in engineering.
2 Could you complete this application ...., please?
3 I'd like to apply for a training .... in computers.
4 You have to take an entrance .... to get into art school.
5 Have you had any work .... in this type of job?
6 I'm going to get a part-time .... two days a week.
7 Excuse me, how much are the course .... ?

2 Choose the correct words to complete the text.

Fraser Doherty ¹(started)/ made his business at the age of 14. He made jam using his grandmother's recipes and sold it to his friends and neighbours and then to supermarkets. As time went on, he ²**developed / started** his jams into a widely recognised brand. He has ³**made / become** a ⁴**millions / millionaire** and his jams have ⁵**made / become** a fortune for his company *SuperJam*. Fraser also ⁶**does / supports** the community through his charity *The SuperJam Tea Parties*, which organises tea parties for lonely elderly people. In 2007, he ⁷**made / won** the ⁸**award / idea** for Global Student Entrepreneur of the Year. And now he looks likely to ⁹**break / win** more records with his new *SuperJam Cookbook*.

3 Complete the sentences with the words in the box. There are two words you don't need to use.

> mix   fry   slice   grate   grill   roast   boil
> ~~bake~~   chop   spread

1 _Bake_ the cake in the oven for 30 minutes.
2 .... the tomatoes into very small pieces.
3 .... the potatoes in half a litre of water.
4 .... the meat in the oven.
5 .... the eggs and the milk in a bowl.
6 .... the mushrooms in some hot oil.
7 .... the tomato sauce over the pizza.
8 .... the mushrooms quite thick.

4 Which adjective in each group can *not* be used to describe the food?

1 ~~crunchy~~ / salty / disgusting
2 sweet / bland / delicious 
3 savoury / slimy / crunchy 
4 bitter / bland / salty 
5 delicious / bitter / slimy 
6 crunchy / spicy / sweet 
7 slimy / sweet / disgusting 
8 salty / bitter / sweet 

Explore vocabulary

5 Complete the sentences with the correct form of *take* and the words in the box.

> advice   time   up   ~~exam~~   place

1 When are you going to _take_ your _exam_ ?
2 I'm not in a hurry – I'm going to .... my ....
3 Listen to me! You should .... my ....
4 I'm .... a new hobby – cookery!
5 When are the job interviews going to .... ?

6 Choose the correct words to complete the text.

Street food is popular in many countries and it is eaten ¹**by / in** a number of different ways. Fishballs are popular ²**on / to** the streets of Bangkok. In La Paz, a city surrounded ³**in / by** mountains, a popular snack is grilled meat with spicy peanut sauce. Everyone has time for some street food, even when they are ⁴**in / on** the go.

50

Language focus

1 Complete the conversation with the correct future form of the verbs in brackets.

Abby: What ¹ *are you doing* (you/do) this evening?
Clare: I ² .... (see) a play at the theatre. It ³ .... (start) at 7.30 pm but I ⁴ .... (meet) Julie for dinner at 6 pm. Why don't you come?
Abby: I'd love to, but I ⁵ .... (catch) a plane early tomorrow, so I ⁶ .... (have) an early night.
Clare: A plane? ⁷ .... (you/go) somewhere nice?
Abby: Yes! I ⁸ .... (do) a tour of Italy. It ⁹ .... (start) in Venice and ¹⁰ .... (end) up in Naples.
Clare: Sounds wonderful! Have a good time!

2 Put the words in order to make predictions.

1 they / in a few weeks / going / the award winners / announce / to / are *They are going to announce the award winners in a few weeks.*
2 watching / the ceremony / everyone / be / on TV / will
3 first prize / I'm / Emma / sure / win / will
4 going / winning £10,000 / make / to her life / is / to / a huge difference
5 anymore / won't / have / she / worry / to / money / about
6 might / school / leave / her own restaurant / she / start / and

3 Choose the correct words to complete the text.

When you ¹(visit)/ 'll visit Australia, you ²want / 'll want to try some of our delicious local dishes. Are you a meat eater? If you ³like / 'll like burgers, you ⁴love / 'll love our kangaroo meat burgers. If you ⁵'re / 'll be a vegetarian, you ⁶prefer / 'll prefer our barbecued corn burgers. We're also famous for our beach barbecues. But remember, you ⁷get / 'll get sunburn if you ⁸don't / won't wear sun cream and a hat. And you ⁹need / 'll need lots of insect spray unless you ¹⁰want / 'll want to end up as dinner for the mosquitoes!

4 Match the beginnings and the ends of the sentences.

1 What would you say *b*
2 If you had to give up one kind of food,
3 If I lived in Japan,
4 I might be healthier
5 Would you eat kangaroo meat
6 I wouldn't eat crocodile meat

a I could eat sushi every day.
b if a friend offered you some burned fish for dinner?
c if I were a vegetarian.
d if someone cooked it for you?
e unless I was really, really hungry.
f what would it be?

Language builder

5 Choose the correct words to complete the text.

Chef Luisa's Food Blog

When I ¹ *a* younger, I ² .... like cooking at all. I ³ .... cheese on toast all the time! But after I had taught ⁴ .... to make a few easy dishes, I decided to go to cookery school. I ⁵ .... a chef for ten years now and I love it! I ⁶ .... to Tokyo next week to open our new restaurant there. We ⁷ .... another one in Osaka, too, in a couple of years. If I ⁸ .... time, I ⁹ .... in some of my favourite restaurants there and I ¹⁰ .... learn some new ideas. My new cookbook ¹¹ .... out next spring, so I guess I ¹² .... publicity tours for that. What's my favourite dish? Well, if I ¹³ .... choose just one dish, it ¹⁴ .... lobster risotto.

	a	b	c
1	was	'd been	've been
2	didn't used to	didn't use to	wouldn't
3	'd eat	use to eat	'd eaten
4	ourselves	yourself	myself
5	'd been	've been	'm
6	flew	'll fly	'm flying
7	're going to open	open	'll open
8	'll have	have	'm having
9	'll eat	've eaten	eat
10	can	might	would
11	has come	is coming	came
12	'll be doing	'll be do	did
13	had	could	would
14	's	'll be	'd be

Speaking

6 Choose the correct options to complete the conversations.

A: I was ¹(thinking)/ suggesting of raising money for the cat hospital.
B: ²This is / That's a good idea.

C: ³Finally / Next, you chop the onion.
D: OK, and then?
C: ⁴Then / Firstly, you need to fry it a little.

E: ⁵When / Then it boils, you need to let it cook gently for ten minutes.
F: Right, this is great. Cooking is easy!

G: How ⁶might / shall we decide then?
H: I think the ⁷best / first way is to ask our class.

Say it right!

Unit 1 Sentence stress in the past perfect

1 🔊 1.14 **Listen and repeat.**
1. We hadn't been to a concert before.
2. I'd forgotten about his birthday.

2 🔊 1.15 **Listen and mark the stresses in the sentences.**
1. The show had sold out really quickly.
2. We'd wanted to go to that restaurant for ages.
3. What? He hadn't seen that film? Ever?
4. Lots of other people had arrived before us.
5. I hadn't expected to see him there. What a surprise!

3 🔊 1.15 **Listen, check and repeat.**

4 Practise saying the sentences in Exercise 2 with the correct stress.

Unit 2 Stress and intonation in questions with *How long?*

1 🔊 1.24 **Listen and repeat.**
1. How **long** have you been **play**ing the gui**tar**?
2. How **long** has she been **teach**ing at the **school**?

2 🔊 1.25 **Listen to the questions. Where are the main stresses (↘)?**
1. How long have you been reading that book?
2. How long has she been living in this street?
3. How long has he been working in that shop?
4. How long has it been raining?
5. How long have they been learning French?

3 🔊 1.25 **Listen, check and repeat.**

4 Practise saying the questions in Exercise 2 with the correct stress and intonation.

Unit 3 Contracted forms in the future continuous

1 🔊 1.34 **Listen and repeat.**
1. In 20 years' time, we'**ll** be doing everything via our smartphones.
2. By the end of the next century, we **won't** be driving cars that use petrol.

2 🔊 1.35 **Listen and identify the contracted forms in the sentences.**
1. I will still be studying in 10 years' time.
2. She will be making a lot of money by the time she's 21.
3. There will be people living on the moon in 100 years' time.
4. Very soon, we will be talking to our computers and we will not be using keyboards.
5. He will not be doing voluntary work because he will not have time.
6. You will not be learning English anymore, you will be learning Chinese.

3 🔊 1.35 **Listen, check and repeat.**

4 Practise saying the sentences in Exercise 2 with the contracted forms.

Unit 4 Stress and intonation in second conditional questions

1 🔊 1.44 **Listen and repeat.**
1. What would you **do** if you were **miles** away from home and had **no** money to get a bus?
2. If someone gave you **jelly**fish at a **dinn**er party, what would you **say**?

2 🔊 1.45 **Listen to the questions. Where are the main stresses (↘)?**
1. What would you do if you forgot your mum's birthday?
2. What would you say if a friend asked you to lend her some money?
3. If you could live anywhere in the world, where would you like to live?
4. If you won the lottery, what would you do with the money?
5. What advice would you give to your friend if he was worried about his exams?
6. If you didn't need to study this evening, what would you do instead?

3 🔊 1.45 **Listen, check and repeat.**

4 Practise saying the questions in Exercise 2 with the correct stress and intonation.

This page is intentionally left blank

Grammar reference

Starter Unit

Past simple vs. past continuous
- We use the past simple to talk about completed events and actions in the past.
Daniel visited Italy two years ago.
- We use the past continuous to talk about actions in progress at a certain time in the past.
At eight o'clock, I was waiting for the train.
- We also use the past continuous with *when* and *while* to describe the situation when something happened.
When we arrived, Granddad was sleeping on the sofa.
While we were getting ready to go out, it started raining.

Present perfect and past simple
- We use the past simple to talk about actions and experiences that happened in a time period that has finished.
In 2009, my little sister was born.
- We use the present perfect to talk about experiences and facts in the past that happened in a time period that isn't finished.
She's bought a lot of new clothes this year.
- We also use the present perfect when the exact time of a past action is not mentioned or important.
You've left the light on in your room.

Present perfect with *still*, *yet*, *already* and *just*
- We use *still* with negative verbs to express that something we expected has not happened, but imagine it will happen in the future. We put *still* directly after the subject.
David still hasn't texted me about this weekend.
- We use *yet* with negative verbs to emphasise that something we expected has not happened. We put *yet* after the complete verb phrase.
Lauren hasn't asked her parents about the party yet.
- We also use *yet* in questions to ask about things we don't think have happened.
Have you bought tickets for the football match yet?
- We use *already* to explain that something happened before we expected or to emphasise it has happened. We usually put *already* between *have/has* and the past participle.
Hurry up! James and Lily have already arrived.
- We use *just* with the present perfect to talk about very recent events and actions. We put *just* between *have/has* and the past participle.
I've just heard that you won the race. Well done!

Word order in questions
- We form most questions with (question word) + auxiliary verb + subject + main verb phrase.
How long do they spend online every day?
Are you going to the concert with friends tomorrow?
- When we form questions with *be* in the present and past simple, we use (question word) + *be* + subject.
Where were you yesterday?
Are you worried about something?

Subject/object questions
- We don't use an auxiliary verb when the question word is the subject.
Who gave you that pen? ('Karl gave me it.')
What makes you happy? ('Spending time with my friends makes me happy.')
- We use an auxiliary verb when the question word is not the subject.
What did you do at the weekend? ('We went shopping and for a pizza.')
Who do you want to win the football match? ('I want Liverpool to win.')

Present perfect with *ever*, *never*, *for* and *since*
- We often use *ever* in present perfect questions when the exact time isn't important. We put *ever* directly after the subject.
Has she ever helped you with your homework?
- We often use *never* to say 'not at any time'. We put *never* between *have/has* and the past participle.
He's never been to New York.
- We use *for* and *since* with the present perfect to say how long something has been true. We use *for* with periods of time, and *since* with a reference to a specific time.
She's lived here for seven years.
He's worked here since 2007.

Present perfect questions
- To form questions in the present perfect, we use (question word) + *have/has* + subject + past participle.
Has John asked you about borrowing your sleeping bag?
Why have you brought sandwiches?
Have they arrived yet?
Have you ever been to Australia?
How long has she lived in Brazil?

Grammar reference

Unit 1

used to and would

+	I/You/He/She/It/We/You/They	used to / would	wear jeans.
−	I/You/He/She/It/We/You/They	didn't use to / wouldn't	wear jeans.
?	Did	I/you/he/she/it/we/you/they	use to	wear jeans?
+	Yes,	I/you/he/she/it/we/you/they		did.
−	No,	I/you/he/she/it/we/you/they		didn't.

- *used to* emphasises that past habits and states are now finished.
  They used to go swimming on Tuesdays.
- We use *would* to describe past habits, but not states.
  When I was a baby, my parents would take me for a walk every afternoon.
  You used to have a ponytail. ~~You would have a ponytail.~~
- We do **not** use *used to* or *would* to talk about things that only happened once, or to say how many times something happened.
  Last year, I went to France. ~~Last year, I used to go to France.~~
  Yesterday, I called him three times. ~~Yesterday, I would call him three times.~~
- We put question words at the beginning of the question.
  What games would you play when you were younger?

1 Write sentences about Chloe's grandmother using *used to* and *didn't use to*.

Chloe's grandmother was a punk, but her life is different now. In the 1970s, she …

> ~~wore tight trousers.~~ had pink hair.
> shocked people.   broke the rules.

Now, she…

> ~~wears long dresses.~~ likes gardening.
> bakes cakes.   follows the rules.

She used to wear tight trousers.
She didn't use to wear long dresses.

2 Rewrite the sentences in Exercise 1 with *would*. If *would* is not possible, write ✗.

She would wear tight trousers.

Past perfect

+	I/You/He/She/It/We/You/They	had	expected it.
−	I/You/He/She/It/We/You/They	hadn't	expected it.
?	Had	I/you/he/she/it/we/you/they	expected it?
+	Yes,	I/you/he/she/it/we/you/they	had.
−	No,	I/you/he/she/it/we/you/they	hadn't.

- We form the past perfect with *had* + past participle.
  I'd seen the film before, so I was bored.
- We use the past perfect when we are talking about the past, but want to go back to an earlier time.
  Jack didn't want to come with us because he'd been there last year.
- We do **not** use the past perfect simply because something happened a long time ago. We use it with other past tenses to make the order things happened clear.
  Ashley didn't get the email because I had typed Ash_55, not Ash-55.
- We put question words at the beginning of the question.
  How far had you walked before you realised you were lost?

3 Complete the sentences with the past perfect form of the verbs in the box.

> go   ~~not tell~~   not win   not meet
> miss   not remember

1 I didn't know. You *hadn't told* me.
2 My aunt wasn't at home. She …. out.
3 He didn't have a present for me. He …. my birthday.
4 I met Ann for the first time last week. I …. her before.
5 It was the first game we won. We …. a game before.
6 Judit arrived late. She …. the 7 o'clock train.

4 Write past perfect questions with the prompts. Answer them using the information in brackets.

1 he / receive / your email? (✗)
  Had he received your email? No, he hadn't.
2 you / save / some money? (✓)
3 she / bring / her skateboard? (✗)
4 Where / had / they / be? (shopping)
5 you / hear / of that book? (✗)
6 What / had / the dog / eat? (my shoes!)

Grammar reference

Unit 2
Reflexive pronouns and *each other*

Subject pronoun	Object pronoun	Reflexive pronoun
I	me	myself
you	you	yourself/yourselves
he	him	himself
she	her	herself
it	it	itself
we	us	ourselves
they	them	themselves

- We use reflexive pronouns when the subject and the object of a verb are the same.
  I sing to myself when I'm alone. ~~I sing to me when I'm alone.~~
- Some of the most common verbs we use with reflexive pronouns are *enjoy*, *hurt*, *teach* and *introduce*.
  They didn't really enjoy themselves at the concert.
- When we use some verbs with reflexive pronouns, they have a different meaning.
  Help yourself to sandwiches! (Take what you want or need.)
  He found himself in a difficult situation. (He didn't intend to be in a difficult situation, but he was.)
- We use *each other* when each of the two (or more) subjects do the verb to the other subject(s).
  José and Rosa sent each other Valentine's cards. (José sent Rosa a Valentine's card, and Rosa sent José a Valentine's card.)

1 Complete the sentences with reflexive pronouns or *each other*.
1. Thank you. I really enjoyed *myself* yesterday.
2. They email …. every day.
3. Our cat hurt …. when it jumped off the roof.
4. Emily and Ryan said goodbye to …. .
5. She introduced …. , and asked me for my name.
6. Sometimes you talk to …. , but don't realise.

Present perfect simple

- We can use the present perfect simple to say how many times we've done something or how much we have completed of something before, and including, now.
  You've looked at those jeans twice. Why don't you buy them?
  Ashley's read all the books in the series.
- We often use time expressions such as *since*, *recently*, *this week/month*, *in the last year* and *today* as these include past and present time.
  I haven't watched TV much recently.
- We often use the present perfect simple to say how many times we have done something.
  I've been to New York three times.

2 Complete the sentences with the present perfect simple form of the verbs in brackets.
1. You *'ve forgotten* (forget) your password twice this week.
2. Julio …. (be) late for school a few times recently.
3. We …. (not study) any algebra this year.
4. How many of the biscuits …. (you/have)?
5. Sorry, I …. (not see) her today.
6. We …. (watch) the first and second series, but not the new one yet.

Present perfect continuous

+	I/We/You/They	have	been having lessons for two years.
	He/She/It	has	
–	I/We/You/They	haven't	been having lessons for two years.
	He/She/It	hasn't	
?	Have	I/we/you/they	been having lessons?
	Has	he/she/it	
+	Yes, I/we/you/they	have.	Yes, he/she/it has.
–	No, I/we/you/they	haven't.	No, he/she/it hasn't.

- We use the present perfect continuous to talk about a series of actions that started in the past, is still in progress and we expect to continue.
  Daniel and Jake have been emailing me about it.
- We often use the present perfect continuous to say how long we have been doing something.
  I've been going to piano lessons for nine years.
- We don't use continuous tenses like the present perfect continuous with state verbs.
  Emily's liked him since she met him. ~~Emily's been liking him since she met him.~~
- We put question words at the beginning of the question.
  Where have you been downloading the music from?

3 Write present perfect continuous questions and answers with the prompts.
1. How long / you / be / sing in the choir?
   I / sing in the choir / couple of months.
   How long have you been singing in the choir?
   I've been singing in the choir for a couple of months.
2. Where / you / go / for French lessons?
   I / go / a language school near the library.
3. you / watch / his video blogs?
   Yes / I / watch / them / since the beginning.
4. Who / teach / her?
   A family friend / teach / her.
5. How long / they / see / each other?
   They / see / each other / about two months.

Grammar reference

Unit 3

be going to and present tenses for the future

+	I	'm		
	He/She/It	's		
	We/You/They	're		help him.
−	I	'm not	going to	
	He/She/It	isn't		
	We/You/They	aren't		
?	Am	I		
	Is	he/she/it		help him?
	Are	we/you/they		

- We use *be going to* to talk about future actions we intend to do.
  I'm not going to go out this weekend.
- We use the present continuous to talk about future arrangements when they have a fixed date.
  My cousin and his girlfriend are getting married in July.
- We use the present simple to talk about scheduled future events including timetables and calendars.
  The train leaves at 7 o'clock on Saturday. Don't be late!

1 Choose the correct options to complete the conversation.

> Kayla: It's your birthday next week. ¹(Are you doing) / Do you do anything special?
> James: Yes, a few of us ²go / are going to the cinema.
> Kayla: What ³you are going / are you going to see?
> James: Probably *A Good Day* – it ⁴'s starting / starts at 9 o'clock, but we ⁵'re meeting / meet at 7.30. We still haven't decided what ⁶we're going to / are we going to do until the film starts. Would you like to come with us?

Predictions with *be going to*, *will* and *may/might*

- We make predictions with *be going to* when we feel we have evidence for our prediction.
  I saw the weather forecast this morning. It's going to rain this weekend.
- We make predictions with *will/won't* when we feel sure about a future action or event. We often use *will/won't* with expressions like *I think*, *I'm sure* and *I expect*.
  I don't think I'll win, but I expect I'll finish in the top ten.
- We use *may* (*not*) or *might* (*not*) to show that we feel less sure, but think a future action or event is probable.
  I might not go to university, so I may get a job with my dad.
- We use the infinitive without *to* with *will* and *may/might*.
  He might come. He might to come.

2 Match the sentences.

1 I'm sure your parents   *c*
2 I feel really ill after that burger.
3 They might need some volunteers at the Christmas market.
4 It's only my opinion, but
5 We may go to visit my uncle this weekend.
6 The doctor said that the problem

a I can ask my dad. He knows the organiser.
b My mum was talking about it last night.
c will understand it was an accident.
d is going to get worse before it gets better.
e Quick! I'm going to be sick.
f I think it'll be great fun.

Future continuous

+	I/You/He/She/It/We/You/They	will	be celebrating.
−	I/You/He/She/It/We/You/They	won't	be celebrating.
?	Will	I/you/he/she/it/we/you/they	be celebrating?
+	Yes,	I/you/he/she/it/we/you/they	will.
−	No,	I/you/he/she/it/we/you/they	won't.

- We use the future continuous to talk about actions we believe will be in progress at a future time.
  In five years, I'll be living in London and working as an engineer.
  By 2025, everyone will be wearing smart watches.
- We put question words at the beginning of the question.
  What will you be doing in ten years' time?
  When will computers be cooking dinner for us?

3 Complete the predictions with the future continuous form of the verbs in brackets.

1 We *'ll be using* (use) digital money on our smartphones, not real money.
2 We …. (not use) passwords to go on websites.
3 Cars …. (drive) themselves automatically.
4 Nobody …. (eat) fast food.
5 People …. (not watch) reality TV shows.
6 …. (we/upload) information directly from our brains to computers?

Grammar reference

Unit 4
First conditional with *if*, *when* and *unless*

Situation	Consequence
(*if* + present simple)	(*will/won't/may/might* + infinitive)
+ If you make lunch,	I'll cook dinner.
− If you don't make lunch,	I won't cook dinner.

Consequence	Situation
(*will/won't/may/might* + infinitive)	(*if* + present simple)
+ I'll cook dinner	if you make lunch.
− I won't cook dinner	if you don't make lunch.

- We use the first conditional to talk about possible situations in the present or future and say what we think the consequences will be.
- We use *if* + present simple (affirmative or negative) to describe the possible action or event.
  If I eat cheese, I won't be able to sleep.
- When we are certain the future event will happen, we use *when*, not *if*.
  When we get home, I'll look for information on the website.
- We can use *unless* to say *except if*. We usually use a positive verb after *unless*.
  If Dad isn't busy at work, he'll be home at 6.30.
  Unless Dad is busy at work, he'll be home at 6.30.
- We use *will* (*not*) when we are sure of the consequence.
  You'll learn lots of good English expressions if you watch films and TV series.
- We use *may/might* (*not*) to show we are less sure about the consequence.
  If we go out for dinner, I may have steak or I might have fish. I don't know!
- When we use *if*, *when* or *unless* to start the sentence, we use a comma between the two parts.
  When I finish my homework, I'll help Olivia with hers.

1 Complete the sentences with the correct form of the verbs in brackets.

1. I might cook pasta tonight if you *want* (want).
2. He's not sure, but he …. (ask) Hannah if she wants to go.
3. I won't enter the competition unless you …. (promise) to help me.
4. When I go on the website, I …. (check) the time of the concert.
5. Unless we start work now, we …. (not finish) before 6 o'clock.

Second conditional with *could* and *might*

Imaginary situation	Possible consequence
(*if* + past simple)	(*would/might/could* + infinitive)
+ If I knew him,	I would/might/could ask him.
− If I didn't know him,	I wouldn't / might not / couldn't ask him.

Possible consequence	Imaginary situation
(*would/might/could* + infinitive)	(*if* + past simple)
+ I would/might/could ask him	if I knew him.
− I wouldn't / might not / couldn't ask him	if I didn't know him.

- We use the second conditional to talk about imaginary situations and the possible consequences.
- We use *if* + past simple (affirmative or negative) to describe the imaginary situation.
  I wouldn't say no if you wanted to borrow my blue shoes.
- We can use *was* or *were* in the *if* part of the sentence with *I*, *he/she* and *it*.
  If it wasn't/weren't so spicy, I'd be able to finish it.
- We can use *unless* to say *except if*. We usually use a positive verb after *unless*.
  I wouldn't eat jellyfish unless you tried it first.
- We use *would* (*not*) when we are sure of the imaginary consequence.
  Michael would get better grades if he didn't spend all his time playing computer games.
- We use *might* (*not*) to show we are less sure about the imaginary consequence.
  If I had more free time, I might take up the guitar.
- We use *could* (*not*) to express a possible imaginary consequence.
  If it was Saturday, we could go out for pizza.
- We can form questions about the imaginary results of imaginary situations with *if* + past simple, (question word) + *would/could* (*not*) + subject + infinitive. We don't usually form questions with *might*.
  If I broke your mobile, would you be angry with me?
  How long would they need to get here if we called them now?

2 Correct the error in each sentence.

1. If we ~~wouldn't~~ go to the party, Laura would be disappointed. *didn't*
2. If she asked me to be a volunteer, I might to say yes.
3. He'll make a fortune if he started selling his paintings.
4. If you cook steak, I wouldn't eat it.
5. Could you walk to school if you would move house?

Vocabulary Bank

UNIT 1

Jog your memory!

1 Cover the words. How many words under each heading can you remember?
Clothes
Adjectives and dependent prepositions

Clothes (page 9)

a baggy jumper	a leather jacket
a cool T-shirt	a silk scarf
a denim skirt	a stripy shirt
a fitted coat	flat shoes
a flowery dress	tight jeans

1 Look at the words in the box. Look at the questions and write sentences.
   1 What clothes do you like wearing?
   2 What are your favourite items of clothing?
   3 What sorts of clothes don't you like wearing?

2 Compare your sentences with a partner.

Adjectives and dependent prepositions (page 12)

afraid of	happy with
disappointed by	interested in
excited about	keen on
fascinated by	proud of

1 Look at the words in the box. Write true and false sentences for you using the adjectives and prepositions.
I'm fascinated by time travel.

2 Work with a partner. Say your sentences and guess which are true and which are false.

Explore compound nouns (page 15)

guitar	style
motor	taxi
street	telephone

band	corners
box	fare
changes	industry

1 Look at the words in the boxes. Match them to make compound nouns.

2 How many other compound nouns can you remember with the words in the first box? Look back at page 15 and check your answers.

3 Use a dictionary to find other compound nouns with the words in the first box.

*telephone book (n)
a big book with a list
of telephone numbers
for …*

Study tip

Use a dictionary to expand your vocabulary and check your spelling.

Vocabulary Bank 107

Vocabulary Bank

UNIT 2

🧠 Jog your memory!

1 Cover the words. How many words under each heading can you remember?
Personal qualities
Phrasal verbs (learning and socialising)

Personal qualities (page 19)

determined	passionate about
easy-going	shy
hard-working	sociable
impatient	strict
motivated	talented

1 Look at the words in the box. Write sentences about your friends and family.
My sister is a very determined person but she can be very impatient too.

2 Work with a partner. Talk about people you know.

🔍 Explore word building (page 20)

challenge	challenging
determination	determined
flexibility	flexible
happiness	happy
passion	passionate
success	successful

1 Look at the words in the box. Which column is nouns and which column is adjectives? Check the meaning of any words you can't remember in a dictionary.

Phrasal verbs (learning and socialising) (page 22)

bring	give	set
count	look	sign
get	pass	

on	on with	together	up	up to

1 Turn to page 22. Look at the phrasal verbs for one minute.

2 Can you remember them all? Match the words in the boxes to make phrasal verbs.

2 Look at the words below. Use a dictionary to find the noun or adjective form for each word.
1 respect (n)   2 trust (n)   3 difficult (adj)

3 Write sentences that are true for you using nouns and adjectives from Exercise 1.
My Maths homework is usually very challenging.

trust (n)
We were wrong to trust him.

📓 Study tip

Use a dictionary to check the different forms a word has. It will help you to use them correctly.

Vocabulary Bank

UNIT 3

🧠 Jog your memory!

1 Cover the words. How many words under each heading can you remember?
Training and qualifications
Achievements

Training and qualifications (page 31)

| application form |
| career path |
| entrance exam / fees |
| part-time course |
| training course |
| university course / degree / exam / fees |
| work experience |

1 Look at the words in the box. Choose a word. Don't tell your partner. Describe the word. Can your partner guess what it is?
You need to complete one of these to get a job.

Achievements (page 34)

become	a business
break	a fortune
develop	a millionaire
do	a project
make	awards
start	records
support	the community
win	voluntary work

1 Look at the words in the boxes. Match them to make collocations.

2 Look back at page 34 and check your answers.

🔍 Explore expressions with *take* (page 32)

take advice	take time
take exams	take up
take place	

1 Look at the words in the box. Write an example sentence for three of the expressions.
You should take your time when you do your homework or you'll make a mistake.

2 Look at the words below. Choose the correct word to make three more expressions with *take*.

| pleasure in | to | seriously |

1 I take my homework very …. – I spend two hours each night doing it.
2 I don't like James – I think he takes …. hurting people.
3 Alice has taken …. high school really well – she absolutely loves it.

take something seriously.
Harry takes his job very seriously.

📝 Study tip

Use your dictionary to find examples of other common collocations and expressions.

Vocabulary Bank 109

Vocabulary Bank

UNIT 4

Jog your memory!

1 Cover the words. How many words under each heading can you remember?
Cooking verbs
Adjectives describing food

Cooking verbs (page 41)

bake	mix
boil	roast
chop	slice
fry	spread
grate	
grill	

bread	garlic
butter	onion
cake	pasta
cheese	sauce
chicken	steak
eggs	tomatoes

1 Look at the words in the boxes. Write sentences about food you like or don't like to eat and cook using words from each box.
My mum bakes wonderful cakes – I love them!
I don't like chopping onions – they make me cry!

2 Compare your list with your partner. Talk about your favourite food.

Adjectives describing food (page 44)

bitter	salty
bland	savoury
crunchy	slimy
delicious	spicy
disgusting	sweet

1 Look at the words in the box. Write sentences that are true for you using the words.
I love spicy Indian food – it's delicious.

2 Turn to page 44 and check that the meaning of your sentences is correct.

3 Compare your sentences with a partner.

Explore prepositional phrases (page 47)

| different ways   the go   the streets   surrounded |

1 Look at the words in the box. Write the words in the correct column.

by	in	on

2 Add these words to the correct column.

| 10 minutes | danger | fire | New Zealand | walk |
| 5 o'clock | depends | influenced | the menu | your country |

3 Look at the text on page 47. How many of the prepositional phrases can you find there? Check the others in a dictionary.

on the streets
time

Study tip

Write prepositional phrases in your notebook with the preposition in a different colour. It will help you to remember them.

1 CLIL

Social Science The history of jeans

THE **AVERAGE AMERICAN** OWNS **SEVEN** PAIRS OF JEANS.

1 💬 Work with a partner. Look at the photo and the fact. Answer the questions.
1. Why do you think jeans are so popular?
2. How many pairs of jeans do you own?
3. In your family, who wears jeans and who doesn't? When do they wear them?

2 🔊 1.48 Read the study notes about jeans in the 20th century. Which fact(s) do you find most surprising?

1900 Jeans were the ideal clothes for low-paid cowboys and miners in the American West, where conditions were hard. Jeans were cheaper and lasted longer than other trousers. This was important for poor, hard-working men.

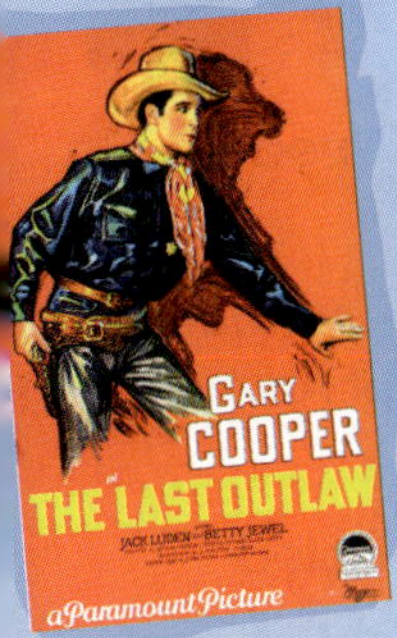

1920s Hollywood films turned cowboys into heroes. Hollywood gave life in the American West a more attractive image. Middle-class Americans wanted to copy what they saw in the films.

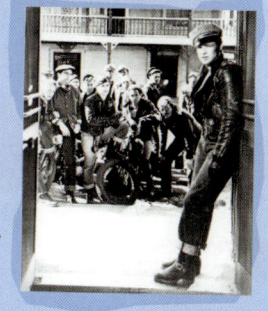

1950s Film stars such as Marlon Brando and James Dean wore jeans on screen and set the fashion for teenagers. Teenagers wanted to show they were different from their parents and they used jeans to do this. Jeans turned into such a strong symbol of rebellion that some schools, cinemas and restaurants banned them.

1960s Hippies wore jeans to show they were the same as the working classes and also to break racial barriers. Hippies wanted all people to be equal.

1970s Better transport routes between countries meant that jeans were manufactured cheaply and prices fell. More people could afford to buy them and jeans became an everyday item of clothing all around the world.

3 Read the text again and answer the questions.
1. Why were jeans the perfect clothes for difficult working conditions?
2. How did Hollywood first help to make jeans popular?
3. Why did teenagers copy the style of film stars?
4. What did hippies hope to achieve by wearing jeans?
5. What happened to the price of jeans when international transport became easier?

4 🔊 1.49 Listen to a teacher and a group of students. What factors influenced who wore jeans?

5 🔊 1.49 Work with a partner. Do you remember what they said about each of the following areas? Listen again and check your answers.
- The economy
- The film industry
- The roles of men and women
- Class
- The environment

Your turn

6 Work with a partner. Choose an item which you think reflects the 20th century and use it to help you talk about social changes. Use the areas in Exercise 5 to help you.

Learn about young trendsetters.
- What do companies want to know about the two trendsetters, Saeko and Yuko?
- What new product are the girls trying out?
- What do they like about the new product?

Discovery EDUCATION

1.4 Trendsetters

2 CLIL

Technology The changing classroom

1 Work with a partner. Make a list of all the technology you use during a school day, from when you wake up to when you go to bed.

2 🔊 1.50 Read the information about flipped classrooms. How many of the things on your list from Exercise 1 are mentioned? Can you add anything to your list?

WHAT IS A FLIPPED CLASSROOM?

In flipped classrooms the students learn on their own at home by watching videos online. These may be videos made by the teacher or the teacher may recommend videos which already exist online and are available to anyone, such as those on online learning websites, like the famous Khan Academy. Later, students do their homework in the classroom, where other students and the teacher can help with any problems. In class, teachers are available to lead classroom debates or explain anything the students did not understand.

Positive things teachers and students say about flipped classrooms:

- Students study at their own speed.
- Teachers have more time to help students one-to-one and give feedback.
- Teachers can use podcasts, chat rooms and apps to make the online lessons more interesting.
- As many teenagers now have their own mobile devices, students can watch the videos anywhere. This has given teenagers the freedom to organise their time in a new way.

3 Read the information again and discuss the questions with a partner.
1 Do you think you would learn more easily in a flipped classroom?
2 Can you think of any disadvantages about learning in a flipped classroom?

4 🔊 1.51 Listen to a student's presentation about online learning videos. Why does she use the videos?

5 🔊 1.51 Listen again and complete the fact file.

THE Khan Academy

Started by: Sal Khan

Who it helps: students from [1] .... with their studies

Languages it's available in: translated into [2] ....

Subjects available: wide range of school subjects, including Maths, History of Art, Physics

Users: school students, home-schooled students, teachers and [3] ....

What it offers: free online [4] .... videos and it's a [5] .... virtual classroom

Your turn

6 Work with a partner. Describe your ideal classroom. What kind of technology would you use? When would you use it and what for?

Learn about a modern house of the future.
- Cleopatra can do the work of several different people. Which people?
- What does Cleopatra tell the boy to do at bedtime?
- How much does Cleopatra cost?

Discovery EDUCATION
2.4 The house of the future

3 CLIL

Natural Science The Archimedes' Principle

$FB = mfg$

1 💬 Work with a partner. When you are swimming in a pool, do you feel lighter, heavier or the same as when you are walking on the ground? Can you explain why?

2 🔊 1.52 Read about Archimedes. What was he trying to find out?

ARCHIMEDES

Archimedes was a Greek mathematician and inventor from the 3rd century BC. He lived in Syracuse and was both friend and relative of King Hiero II, the ruler of Syracuse.

KING HIERO'S PROBLEM
The king thought that his new crown was not made out of solid gold. He thought it had probably been made out of silver then covered in gold. The king asked Archimedes to find out but told him he couldn't damage the crown.

ARCHIMEDES' PROBLEM
Archimedes knew that to see if the crown was pure gold he could not just weigh the crown. He had to know both the volume and the weight of the crown. A crown made of solid gold would have the same volume as pure gold of the same weight. His problem was how to calculate the volume of an irregularly shaped object.

ARCHIMEDES' SOLUTION
He realised that if he could measure the amount of water the crown displaced, he'd be able to calculate its volume. He put the crown in water. Then he put pure gold of the same weight in water and measured the amount of water that was spilled by each object.

THE RESULTS
The crown and the pure gold displaced different amounts of water. Archimedes now knew the weight of both objects and the volume of both objects.

THE CONCLUSION
Although the crown and the quantity of pure gold weighed the same they did not have the same volume and therefore could not be the same material. The king's crown was not made of solid gold.

Archimedes was in fact investigating the density of the material the crown was made of and comparing it to the density of solid gold. Density is calculated by dividing the weight of an object by its volume.

3 Read the article again. Are these sentences true or false? Correct the false sentences.
1. The king was not sure exactly what his crown was made out of.
2. Archimedes calculated the crown's volume by measuring the amount of water it displaced.
3. The crown and the pure gold displaced equal amounts of water.
4. The crown was made of pure gold.
5. Density is calculated by adding the object's weight and volume.

Your turn

4 Work in pairs. What do you know about what these scientists studied and their achievements?

> Charles Darwin   Marie Curie   Galileo Galilei
> Albert Einstein   Isaac Newton

Learn about global warming.
- How old is Eric Gustavsson?
- What will be different about each box?
- What does Eric think his experiment shows?

Discovery EDUCATION

3.4 A cool experiment

4 CLIL

Technology Vertical farming

1 💬 Work with a partner. Look at the problems connected with a growing global population and discuss possible solutions.

> more houses means fewer green spaces
> more people need more food
> a bigger population produces more pollution

2 🔊 1.53 Read the information about vertical farming. What is the main difference between vertical farming and traditional farming?

VERTICAL FARMING: the up-and-coming solution

When it is difficult to find space to build more houses and offices, we automatically build upwards; we build skyscrapers. Now, some farmers are farming upwards too.

What is vertical farming?
Vertical farms save space by growing **plants** inside buildings on specially designed racks. Each **rack** can hold many **plants** and this increases the amount of food produced.

The technology that makes it possible
Hydroponics is a system where special **water** is given to the plants; water which contains everything the plant needs to grow. In traditional farming, plants grow in the ground but in vertical farms plants grow in **pots** and are only fed with special water. Some farmers have racks attached to elevators. Because the elevators are always moving, the plants are always moving too. In this way the plants receive lots of **sunlight** and grow better.

The benefits
Vertical farming works well because farmers have full control of the growing conditions. They control temperature, food and water; so vertical farmers can grow crops all year long and almost anywhere in the world. Furthermore, vegetables grown in the city do not have to be transported as far to reach the shops. This means the food is delivered fresher and with less transport, so there is less pollution.

3 Complete the diagram of a vertical farm with the words in bold from the text.

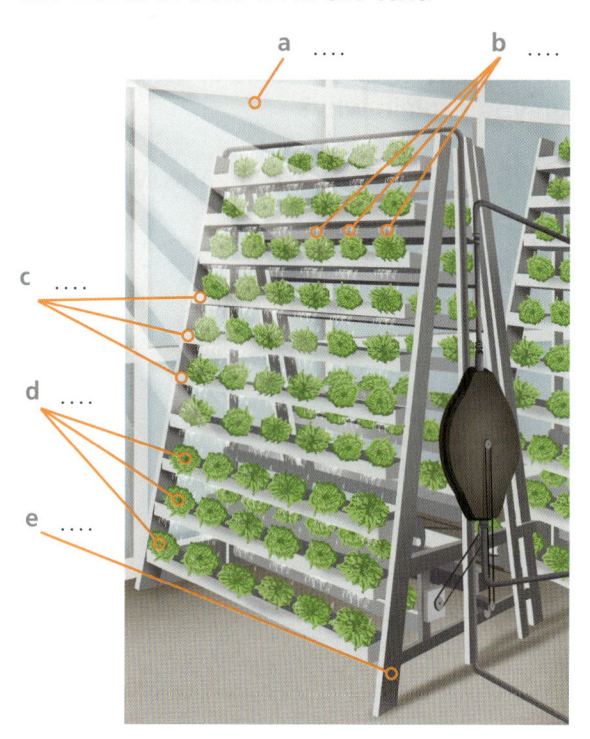

a ....
b ....
c ....
d ....
e ....

4 🔊 1.54 Listen to a radio interview with a vertical farmer. His farm helps in two important ways – what are they?

5 🔊 1.54 Listen again and answer the questions.
1 What would have happened to the factory if Dan hadn't started his vertical farm?
2 What is important about where his factory is?
3 Where does he sell his fruit and vegetables?

Your turn

6 Work with a partner. Many people in the world don't have enough food. Discuss with a partner how vertical farming could help to solve this problem.

Learn about how we can eat healthily.
• Why do factories change food?
• What should we check when we buy food?
• What makes fruit tasty?

Discovery EDUCATION

4.4 You are what you eat

Project 1

A presentation

Stephen Sutton
'An inspiration'
Stephen believed that living a long time was less important than doing something exceptional with the time you have.

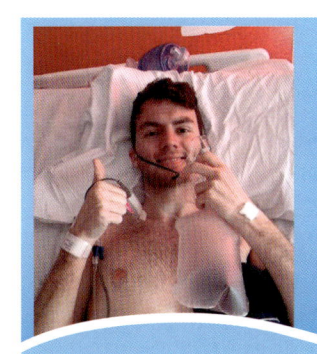

Life
Born in 1994 in the UK
Excellent student and sportsman
Diagnosed with cancer aged 15
Died aged 19

Achievements
Started blog and #thumbsupforstephen fundraising campaign for Teenage Cancer Trust
Raised almost £5 million for charity
Awarded MBE by Queen Elizabeth II

My young achiever is Stephen Sutton. He was called an inspiration by many people who knew him. Here you can see the way he thought about life. He suffered from cancer for four years but never felt sorry for himself. He dedicated his life to raising money for teenage cancer sufferers.
He was born in England in 1994. He was a healthy, active schoolboy ... He ...

Look

1 **Look at the presentation about Stephen Sutton. Answer the questions.**
   1 Did Stephen have a normal life?
   2 Why was he called an inspiration?

2 **Work with a partner. Based on the presentation in Exercise 1, tick the sentences which describe how to give a good presentation.**
   1 You should put everything you are going to say on the presentation slides or cards.
   2 You need about 20 slides for a good presentation.
   3 An image on each slide makes the presentation interesting.
   4 The slides should only contain key words or short notes.
   5 Three to five slides are enough for this topic.
   6 You need to write the details about the key words or notes on paper, ready to say them to your audience.
   7 You can do a presentation using PowerPoint or cards that you print or write on.
   8 You should read everything from the slides.
   9 Give the audience a general idea about the person, then give some biographical details, then talk about their achievements.
   10 The slides should be attractive, without much text but with images to interest and educate the audience.

Prepare

3 **Work in pairs. Choose a famous young person who you admire. It could be a sportsperson, entertainer, writer, etc. or someone brave like Stephen. Use the Internet to research this person. Find out about their background and their main achievements and make notes on these points. You should also include pictures of and, if possible, quotations by this person.**

4 **Prepare your presentation using a software programme like Microsoft PowerPoint or big pieces of card to hold up or stick to the board. Use your notes and pictures from Exercise 3 and the advice from Exercise 2.**

Present

5 **Give your presentation to the class. Remember, you should say most of the information. You only need pictures and main points on the slides. When every pair has finished, have a class vote on which of the young achievers is the most impressive.**

Thanks and acknowledgements

The authors and publishers would like to thank all the teachers and consultants who have contributed to the development of this course, in particular:

Argentina: Fernando Armesto; Natalia Bitar; Verónica Borrás; Leonor Corradi ; Paz Moltrasio; Diana Ogando; Brazil: Dalmo Carvalho; Roberto Costa; Sônia M. B. Leites; Gloria Paz; Litany Pires Ribeiro; Christina Riego; Renata Condi de Souza; Elizabeth White; Chile: Magdalena Aldunate; M. Cristina Darraidou Diaz; Valentina Donoso; Ana María Páez Jofrré; Ricardo Contreras Marambio; Claudia Ottone; Maria Elena Ramirez; Jacqueline Rondon; Alicia Paez Ubilla; Colombia: Luz Amparo Bautista; Sonia Ruiz Hernández; Sandra Jara; Fabian Jimenez; Bibiana Andrea Piñeros Merizalde; Lucero Amparo Bernal Nieto; Olga Olarte; Bibiana Piñeros; Emelis Rambut; Sonia Ruíz; Poland: Anna Bylicka; Russia: Natalya Melchenkova; Irina Polyakova; Svetlana Suchkova; Irina Vayserberg; Turkey: Ali Bilgin; Angela Çakır; Shirley Nuttal; Cinla Sezgin; Mujgan Yesiloglu

The authors and publishers acknowledge the following sources of copyright material and are grateful for the permissions granted. While every effort has been made, it has not always been possible to identify the sources of all the material used, or to trace all copyright holders. If any omissions are brought to our notice, we will be happy to include the appropriate acknowledgements on reprinting.

p. 5 (TR): Getty Images/JGI/Jamie Grill; p. 7 (BR): Alamy/©Jeff Greenberg 6 of 6; p. 8 (B/G): Alamy/©Trevor Mogg; p. 10 (1): Alamy/©Adams Picture Library t/a apl; p. 10 (2): Alamy/©Pictorial Press Ltd; p. 10 (3): Alamy/©PYMCA; p. 11 (4): Alamy/©Trinity Mirror/Mirrorpix; p. 12 (TR): Alamy/©AF archive; p. 12 (CR): Corbis/K. Vreeland; p. 12 (BR): Shutterstock Images/Monkey Business Images; p. 14 (TR): Alamy/©Marka; p. 14 (TC): Shutterstock Images/Stockphoto-graf; p. 14 (TL): Shutterstock Images/Fedorov Oleksiy; p. 15 (TR): Alamy/©Esa Hiltula; p. 15 (L): Shutterstock Images/Luis Santos; p. 15 (CL): Shutterstock Images/Denis Dryashkin; p. 15 (CR): Alamy/©P.D. Amedzro; p. 16 (CR): Alamy/©Jose Luis Pelaez Inc/Blend Images; p. 17 (TL): Getty Images/Olle Lindeborg/AFP; p. 18 (B/G): Shutterstock Imaegs/Jon E Oringer; p. 19 (a): Getty Images/Aminart; p. 19 (b): Alamy/©Hero Images Inc.; p. 19 (c): Getty Images/DragonImages; p. 19 (d): Alamy/©STOCK4B GmbH; p. 19 (e): Alamy/©Bob Ebbesen; p. 20: Darío Rodríguez/DESNIVEL./Courtesy of Robyn Raboutou; p. 22 (TR): Shutterstock Images/Monkey Business Images; p. 24 (TR): Alamy/©Hemis; p. 24 (CR): Alamy/©Top Photo Corporation; p. 24 (T): Alamy/©PS-I; p. 24 (BR): Getty Images/Boaz Rottem; p. 25 (CL): Alamy/©Chao-Yang Chan; p. 25 (BR): Alamy/©Top Photo Corporation; p. 26 (C): Getty Images/Media Photos; p. 27 (TR): Alamy/©Robert Fried; p. 28 (1): Shutterstock Images/Demidoff; p. 28 (2): Shutterstock Images/Maksim Striganov; p. 28 (3): Shutterstock Images/Bestshortstop; p. 28 (4): Shutterstock Images/Ruslan Kudrin; p. 28 (5): Shutterstock Images/Jitinatt Jufask; p. 28 (6): Shutterstock Images/Gordana Sermek; p. 28 (7): Shutterstock Images/Ruslan Kudrin; p. 28 (8): Shutterstock Images/WithGod; p. 29 (TR): Alamy/©Cultura Creative; p. 30 (B/G): Corbis/JOHN VIZCAINO/Reuters; p. 31 (TL): Shutterstock Images/Prasit Rodphan; p. 31 (CL): Alamy/©Boelkow/vario images GmbH & Co.KG; p. 31 (CR): Shutterstock Images/Goodluz; p. 31 (T): Alamy/©Jeff Morgan 16; p. 32 (BR): Alamy/©Juice Images; p. 34 (T): Alamy/©Diana Mewes/Cephas Picture Library; p. 34: Mitchell Robinson; p. 36 (CR): Alamy/©Kevin Allen; p. 36 (B): Alamy/©Tom Salyer; p. 37 (TC): Getty Images/Al Bello; p. 37 (CL): Getty Images/Pamela Martin; p. 37 (CR): Getty Images/Robert Prezioso; p. 38 (CR): Getty Images/Stuart Fox; p. 39 (TR): Getty Images/Huntstock; p. 39 (CR): Getty Images/Chris Ryan; p. 40 (B/G): Getty Images/Ludger Rose/StockFood Creative; p. 41 (a): Shutterstock Images/Joe Belanger; p. 41 (b): Getty Images/Sanapadh; p. 41 (c): Alamy/©MBI; p. 41 (d): Alamy/©FStop Images GmbH; p. 41 (e): Alamy/©Profimedia.CZ a.s.; p. 41 (f): Shutterstock Images/Catalin Petolea; p. 41 (g): Shutterstock Images/Masson; p. 41 (h): Alamy/©Studio51; p. 41 (i): Shutterstock Images/Elena Elisseeva; p. 41 (j): Shutterstock Images/Tagstock1; p. 42 (TR): Getty Images/Nicole S. Young; p. 42 (CL): Shutterstock Images/Peter Zijlstra; p. 42 (CR): Corbis/Eyal Warshavsky/Baubau/ JPN; p. 43 (TL): Shutterstock Images/Luiscar74;

p. 44 (a): Getty Images/C_yung; p. 44 (b): Corbis/Lehmann, Herbert/the food passionates; p. 44 (BC): Getty Images/VM/E+; p. 45 (c): Shutterstock Images/Chad Zuber; p. 46 (T): Shutterstock Images/Sean Pavone; p. 46 (CL): Alamy/©Peter Horree; p. 46 (TCR): Alamy/©Boaz Rottem; p. 46 (BCR): Alamy/©EDU Vision; p. 46 (1): Alamy/©Michael Patrick O'Neill; p. 46 (2): Shutterstock Images/David Salcedo; p. 46 (3): Shutterstock Images/Bluehand; p. 47 (BL): Shutterstock Images/WithGod; p. 47 (BC): Alamy/©Dan Santillo NZ; p. 47 (BR): Getty Images/Maria_Lapina; p. 48 (a): Shutterstock Images/Olga Nayashkova; p. 48 (b): Shutterstock Images/ER_09; p. 48 (c): Getty Images/Alberto gagna; p. 48 (CR): Shutterstock Images/Fanfo; p. 48 (BR): Shutterstock Images/Siamionau pavel; p. 49 (TR): Shutterstock Images/Joe Gough; p. 50 (CL): Alamy/©GARY DOAK; p. 51 (TR): Shutterstock Images/Tyler Olson; p. 52 (B/G): Alamy/©Matthew Chattle; p. 52 (a): Shutterstock Images/Ivaschenko Roman; p. 52 (b): Shutterstock Images/Olga Popova; p. 52 (c): Shutterstock Images/Michael Dechev; p. 52 (d): Shutterstock Images/Cynoclub; p. 52 (e): Shutterstock Images/ILYA AKINSHIN; p. 52 (f): Shutterstock Images/Anaken2012; p. 52 (g): Shutterstock Images/Aksenova Natalya; p. 52 (h): Shutterstock Images/Minerva Studio; p. 52 (i): Shutterstock Images/Filip Bjorkman; p. 52 (j): Shutterstock Images/Chimpinski; p. 54 (T): Corbis/DIVYAKANT SOLANKI/epa; p. 55 (TR): Shutterstock Images/Karkas; p. 55 (CR): Getty Images/Moment; p. 56 (T): Getty Images/Mark Dyball; p. 58 (B): Alamy/©keith morris; p. 59 (TR): Getty Images/PhotoAlto/Frederic Cirou; p. 60 (CR): Alamy/©LearningStockImages; p. 60 (BR): Getty Images/Neil Godwin/Digital Camera Magazine; p. 60 (BL): Alamy/©John Powell/Bubbles Photolibrary; p. 61 (TR): Shutterstock Images/Sompop_Pundrikabha; p. 62 (B/G): Getty Images/Paul Grebliunas; p. 63 (1): Alamy/©Paul Springett C; p. 63 (2): Getty Images/RubberBall Productions, p. 64 (TL): Alamy/©Robert Slade/Manor Photography; p. 64 (CL): Getty Images/iStockphoto; p. 65 (TL): Getty Images/Jutta Klee; p. 66 (a): Alamy/©FocusChina; p. 66 (b): Shutterstock Images/Paolo Bona; p. 67 (c): Alamy/©ZUMA Press, Inc.; p. 67 (CR): Alamy/©Piero Cruciatti; p. 68 (B/G): Alamy/©All Canada Photos; p. 68 (TR): Alamy/©Robert Fried; p. 69 (B): Getty Images/Chung Sung-Jun; p. 69 (CR): Getty Images/Chung Sung-Jun; p. 70 (CR): Getty Images/Stefano Gilera/Cultura; p. 70 (BR): Corbis/Barry Lewis; p. 71 (TR): Getty Images/Hugh Threlfall; p. 72 (1): Alamy/©Chris Howes/Wild Places Photography; p. 72 (2): Alamy/©keith morris; p. 72 (3): Shutterstock Images/Andy Dean Photography; p. 72 (4): Getty Images/David Sacks; p. 72 (5): Getty Images/iStockphoto; p. 72 (6): Alamy/©Kumar Sriskandan; p. 72 (7): Alamy/©Ian Lamond; p. 72 (8): Getty Images/Peter DaSilva; p. 72 (BR): Getty Images/Jupiterimages; p. 73 (TC): Getty Images/verdateo; p. 74 (B/G): Getty Images/Colin Anderson; p. 75 (L): Alamy/©Ben Molyneux; p. 75 (C): Alamy/©Studio Works; p. 75 (R): Alamy/©Helene Rogers/Art Directors & TRIP; p. 78 (T): Getty Images/Jpique; p. 79 (C): Shutterstock Images/Kingarion; p. 79 (CR): Shutterstock Images/Germanskydiver; p. 79 (BC): Alamy/©David Ridley; p. 79 (BR): Getty Images/MANDEL NGAN/Staff; p. 80 (B/G): Alamy/©Deco; p. 80 (TC): Shutterstock Images/Jarno Gonzalez Zarraonandia; p. 80 (TR): Corbis/MARIANA BAZO/X00023/Reuters; p. 80 (CR): Getty Images/GERALDO CASO/AFP; p. 81 (CL): Shutterstock Images/MarclSchauer; p. 81 (CR): Alamy/©Emily Riddell; p. 81 (BR): Alamy/©Jim West; p. 82 (TR): Alamy/©Blend Images; p. 83 (TR): Alamy/©Adrian Sherratt; p. 84 (B/G): Corbis/Charles O'Rear; p. 85 (a): Alamy/©Andriy Kravchenko; p. 85 (b): Shutterstock Images/Photographee.eu; p. 85 (c): Alamy/©imageBROKER; p. 85 (d): Shutterstock Images/Ammentorp Photography; p. 85 (e): Alamy/©Meritzo; p. 85 (f): Getty Images/YinYang; p. 85 (g): Shutterstock Images/Dustie; p. 85 (h): Shutterstock Images/A Lesik; p. 86 (a): Alamy/©Radius Images; p. 86 (b): Alamy/©Michael Sayles; p. 86 (c): Newscom/Europics; p. 89 (B): Getty Images/Image Source; p. 90 (B): Alamy/©Radius Images; p. 91 (TL): Getty Images/Hemera; p. 91 (CL): Getty Images/EyesWideOpen; p. 91 (CR): Alamy/©Kumar Sriskandan; p. 92 (C): Getty Images/Christof Koepsel/Bongarts; p. 93 (TR): Getty Images/Mark Webster; p. 94 (BR): Alamy/©B.O'Kane; p. 108 (TC): Getty Images/DragonImages; p. 108 (TR): Alamy/©STOCK4B GmbH; p. 108 (CR): Alamy/©Hero Images Inc.; p. 109 (TC): Shutterstock Images/Prasit Rodphan; p. 109 (TR): Alamy/©Jeff Morgan 16; p. 110 (TC):

Alamy/©Profimedia.CZ a.s.; p. 110 (TR): Shutterstock Images/Catalin Petolea; p. 110 (C): Alamy/©Studio51; p. 110 (CR): Shutterstock Images/Tagstock1; p. 111 (TC): Shutterstock Images/Cynoclub; p. 111 (TR): Shutterstock Images/Aksenova Natalya; p. 111 (C): Shutterstock Images/Filip Bjorkman; p. 111 (CR): Shutterstock Images/Chimpinski; p. 112 (TC): Alamy/©Paul Springett C; p. 112 (TR): Getty Images/RubberBall Productions; p. 113 (TC): Shutterstock Images/Radu Bercan; p. 113 (TR): Getty Images/KidStock; p. 114 (TR): Shutterstock Images/Dustie; p. 114 (CR): Shutterstock Images/A Lesik; p. 115 (TR): Shutterstock Images/Demidoff; p. 115 (TC): Getty Images/Fotosearch; p. 115 (CL): Alamy/©Pictorial Press Ltd; p. 115 (C): Alamy/©Pictorial Press Ltd; p. 115 (BL): Getty Images/Michael Ochs Archives; p. 115 (BCL): Alamy/©ClassicStock; p. 115 (BCR): Shutterstock Images/Aaron Amat; p. 115 (CR): Shutterstock Images/Ragnarock; p. 115 (BR): Getty Images/SSPL; p. 116 (BL): Getty Images/svetikd/iStockphoto; p. 116 (CR): Getty Images/Neilson Barnard; p. 117 (TR): Getty Images/Hulton Archive/stringer; p. 118 (BL): Rexfeatures/Solent News; p. 119 (BL): Alamy/©Modern Design; p. 120 (CR): Getty Images/The Washington Post; p. 121 (TL): Shutterstock Images/Klagyivik Viktor; p. 121 (CR): Shutterstock Images/Nayneung1; p. 121 (BL): Alamy/©John Warburton-Lee Photography; p. 122 (CR): Alamy/©Tetra Images; p. 122 (CR): Shutterstock Images/alpimages; p. 123 (TL): Newscom/Mirrorpix; p. 123 (TR): AP Images/Stephen Sutton/Press Association; p. 123 (CL): Newscom/SWNS/Splash News.

Front cover photograph by Getty Images/Eduardo Garcia.

The publishers are grateful to the following illustrators:

Anni Betts: p. 35 (2, 3, 4), 95; Q2A Media Services, Inc.: p. 6, 9, 14, 15, 16, 24, 25, 35 (1), 36, 37, 46, 49, 50, 54, 56, 68, 69, 76, 80, 81, 88, 107, 113, 117, 118, 119, 124, 125; Jose Rubio: p. 4, 13, 78.

All video stills by kind permission of:

Discovery Communications, LLC 2015: p. 8 (1, 2, 4), 11, 14, 18 (1, 2, 4), 21, 24, 30 (1, 2, 4), 33, 36, 40 (1, 2, 4), 43, 46, 52 (1, 2, 4), 55, 58, 62 (1, 2, 4), 65, 68, 74 (1, 2, 4), 77, 80, 84 (1, 2, 4), 87, 90, 115, 116, 117, 118, 119, 120, 121, 122; Cambridge University Press: p. 8 (3), 16, 18 (3), 26, 30 (3), 38, 40 (3), 48, 52 (3), 60, 62 (3), 70, 74 (3), 82, 84 (3), 92.

The authors and publishers acknowledge the following sources of copyright material and are grateful for the permissions granted. While every effort has been made, it has not always been possible to identify the sources of all the material used, or to trace all copyright holders. If any omissions are brought to our notice, we will be happy to include the appropriate acknowledgements on reprinting and in the next update to the digital edition, as applicable.

Madison Robinson for the text on p. 34 from *FishFlops® About Us*, http://fishflops.com/madison-nicole-robinson. Reprinted with permission;

Fraser Doherty for the text on p. 50 from *Fraser Doherty: The Adventures of Jam Boy*, www.fraserdoherty.com. Reprinted with permission.

The publisher has used its best endeavours to ensure that the URLs for external websites referred to in this book are correct and active at the time of going to press. However, the publisher has no responsibility for the websites and can make no guarantee that a site will remain live or that the content is or will remain appropriate.

Corpus
Development of this publication has made use of the Cambridge English Corpus (CEC). The CEC is a computer database of contemporary spoken and written English, which currently stands at over one billion words. It includes British English, American English and other varieties of English. It also includes the Cambridge Learner Corpus, developed in collaboration with the University of Cambridge ESOL Examinations. Cambridge University Press has built up the CEC to provide evidence about language use that helps to produce better language teaching materials.

English Profile
This product is informed by the English Vocabulary Profile, built as part of English Profile, a collaborative programme designed to enhance the learning, teaching and assessment of English worldwide. Its main funding partners are Cambridge University Press and Cambridge ESOL and its aim is to create a 'profile' for English linked to the Common European Framework of Reference for Languages (CEF). English Profile outcomes, such as the English Vocabulary Profile, will provide detailed information about the language that learners can be expected to demonstrate at each CEF level, offering a clear benchmark for learners' proficiency. For more information, please visit www.englishprofile.org

The authors and publishers would like to thank a number of people whose support has proved invaluable during the planning, writing and production process of this course.

The publishers are grateful to the following contributors:
Blooberry and emc design ltd: concept design
emc design limited: text design and layouts
QBS Learning: cover design and photo selection
Ian Harker and Dave Morritt at DSound: audio recordings
Integra: video production
Nick Bruckman and People's TV: voxpop video production
Hart McCleod: video voiceovers
Anna Whitcher: video management
BraveArts, S.L: additional audio recordings
Getty Images: music
Vicki Anderson: Speaking and Writing pages
Debbie Owen: Starter Unit
Ruth Appleton: CLIL pages
Mick Green and Ingrid Wisniewska: Grammar Reference pages
Emma Szlachta: Copy editor & Vocabulary Bank
Debbie Owen: Project pages
Tim Foster: Content development and editor

Eyes Open 4
WORKBOOK
COMBO A

Vicki Anderson with Eoin Higgins

CAMBRIDGE UNIVERSITY PRESS

Discovery EDUCATION

Contents

Starter Unit — page 3

1 Trends — page 7

2 A helping hand — page 17

3 Young achievers — page 27

4 Fabulous food — page 37

Speaking extra — page 87

Language focus extra — page 95

Starter Unit

Past simple vs. past continuous

1 ★★ Complete the text with the past simple or past continuous form of the verbs in the box.

> not look decide concentrate still hold
> tell fall arrive pull call walk (x2)
> try notice see

A young man ¹ _was walking_ along the side of the river near his home when he ² _____ to check his Facebook page. Because he ³ _____ on his phone, he ⁴ _____ where he was going and ⁵ _____ into the river. Luckily, a couple who ⁶ _____ on the other side of the river ⁷ _____ what happened, and ⁸ _____ the emergency services. When the rescuers ⁹ _____ to save him, the man ¹⁰ _____ to get out of the water. He ¹¹ _____ them that he couldn't swim. While the rescuers ¹² _____ him out of the water, one of them ¹³ _____ that he ¹⁴ _____ his mobile phone!

Question words

2 ★★ Complete the questions with the words in the box. Then match the questions (1–7) with the answers (a–g).

> Why How When Who Which ~~Where~~ What

1 _Where_ shall we go to have lunch? _e_
2 _____ shop shall we go in next? ___
3 _____ didn't you go on the trip to the castle? ___
4 _____ did you go to the cinema with? ___
5 _____ did the magician do that trick? ___
6 _____ does the library close? ___
7 _____ did you enjoy the most? ___

a I went there last year.
b My sister and my cousins.
c Nine o'clock, I think.
d I loved the karaoke.
e There's a picnic place over there.
f I want to go in the shoe shop.
g No idea, but it was amazing!

-ed and -ing adjectives

3 ★ Circle the correct words.
1 She was so **interested** / interesting in her Facebook posts that she missed her bus stop.
2 Why wasn't she more **worried** / **worrying** about failing the exam?
3 I think speaking in public is a **terrified** / **terrifying** experience, but she's always really calm.
4 I didn't think the museum was **bored** / **boring**! I learned a lot.
5 The boy who rescued the dog had an **excited** / **exciting** story to tell his friends.
6 They all felt very **tired** / **tiring** after the walk.

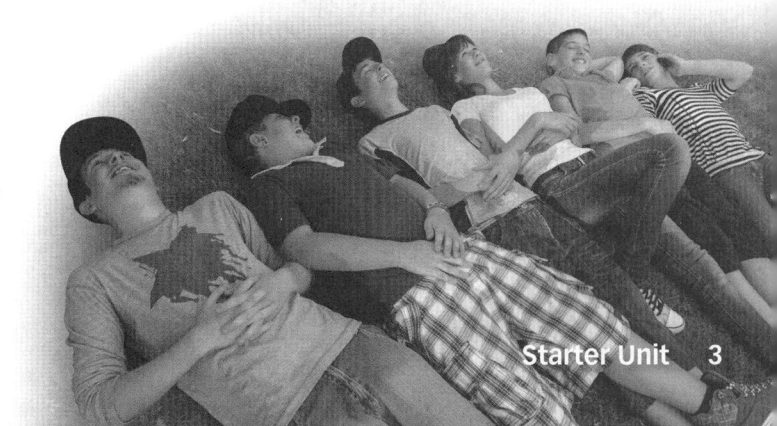

Starter Unit 3

Starter Unit

Phrasal verbs

4 ★ Rewrite the parts of the sentences in *italics* using the phrasal verbs in the box.

> come back   ~~pick up~~   find out
> set off   chill out   look round

1. I can *come and get you* at your house if you like. — *pick you up*
2. It's a big zoo. We need hours to *go and see* every section. _____
3. All our exams are finished, so we can just *relax* this weekend. _____
4. Did you *discover* what time the concert starts tomorrow? _____
5. We *started the journey* at six o'clock in the morning. _____
6. If you don't like working in New York, you can *return* to your job here. _____

Energy issues

5 ★ Find five more verbs for energy issues in the wordsquare. Two of them have prepositions.

w	a	s	t	e	s	k	l
o	v	a	z	a	w	o	e
b	i	v	c	r	i	p	a
a	r	e	d	s	t	u	v
n	e	j	l	h	c	o	e
d	d	r	q	u	h	m	a
t	u	r	n	d	o	w	n
o	c	t	a	p	f	u	n
n	e	x	t	h	f	f	o

6 ★ Complete the sentences with the correct form of the verbs in Exercise 5.

1. If we want to __save__ our planet, we need to use less energy every day.
2. My little brother never _____ the TV when he stops watching it. Why is he so lazy?
3. Can we _____ the air conditioning, please? It's too cold in here!
4. We have managed to _____ how much electricity we use. Now we use 35% less.
5. Paul, you _____ your computer on again when you went out! It's been on all day!
6. We try not to _____ water in our house. We all have short showers, not baths.

Present perfect and past simple

7 ★★ Complete the email with the present perfect or past simple form of the verbs in brackets.

Hi Leona,
How's life back home? We ¹__have been__ (be) on holiday in Amsterdam all week! We ²_____ (set off) for the airport on Sunday morning, but the plane ³_____ (not take off) until the evening because there ⁴_____ (be) a problem with the engine. Finally, we ⁵_____ (arrive) at the apartment at midnight. ☹
⁶_____ (you/go) to Amsterdam? It's an amazing city. Up to now, we ⁷_____ (spend) lots of time just looking round the city centre at all the old houses and canals. Of course, in the last few days my parents ⁸_____ (make) lots of plans for our stay, but now my brother ⁹_____ (decide) he just wants to chill out before he starts university! So yesterday, I ¹⁰_____ (go) on a trip to see some windmills with my parents and he ¹¹_____ (stay) in the apartment. Today we ¹²_____ (book) online tickets for the Van Gogh museum, though, and he is coming with us.
Will write again soon,
Carrie

make and *do*

8 ★ Complete the sentences with *make* or *do*.

1. Be careful or you'll __make__ a mistake.
2. Sssssh! Please don't _____ a noise.
3. Did you _____ anything interesting today?
4. We mustn't _____ a mess.
5. We need to _____ the right thing.
6. I can't _____ a phone call here.
7. It's difficult for some people to _____ friends.
8. Did you _____ all your homework last night?

Starter Unit

Present perfect with *still*, *yet*, *already* and *just*

9 ★ **Complete the sentences with *still*, *yet*, *already* or *just*.**

1 Look, I've ___just___ bought some new football boots. What do you think?
2 **Dad:** Have you switched off your computer _____ ? We're leaving now.
  Ollie: Don't worry, Dad! I've _____ done it. I did it ages ago!
3 Have you bought Kerry a birthday present _____ ?
4 I've _____ packed most of the things we need for the trip, but I haven't found my passport _____ . Have you seen it?
5 **Anna:** Jacinta dropped her bracelet in the garden. She _____ hasn't found it.
  Jacinta: *[in the garden]* Hurray!
  Sue: It sounds like she's _____ found it. Thank goodness for that!

Art around us

10 ★ **Match the words in the box with the definitions. There are two extra words.**

> microphone mural orchestra portrait exhibition gallery juggler sculpture

1 a painting on a wall — ___mural___
2 a place you can see paintings or other art — _____
3 a 3D work of art made from stone, metal or other materials — _____
4 a group of works of art all together, you can see this in 2 above — _____
5 a gadget you sing or play into to make the sound louder — _____
6 a painting of a person — _____

Word order in questions

11 ★ **Put the words in order to make questions.**

1 holiday / going / Who / are / with / you / on / ?
   Who are you going on holiday with?
2 does / the / When / start / safari / ?
   _____
3 see / can / we / there / animals / What / ?
   _____
4 flight / airport / go / does / Which / from / the / ?
   _____
5 did / park / How / get / to / she / safari / the / ?
   _____
6 any / you / lions / yet / seen / Have / ?
   _____

Subject/object questions

12 ★ **Circle the correct words in the table.**

1	In the sentence 'I saw Luis.', Luis is the **subject / object**.
2	In the sentence 'Luis saw me.', Luis is the **subject / object**.
3	In the question 'Who did you see?', 'Who' is the **subject / object**. The answer is: 'I saw Luis.' / 'Luis saw me.'
4	In the question 'Who saw you?', 'Who' is the **subject / object**. The answer is: 'I saw Luis.' / 'Luis saw me.'

13 ★★ **Complete the conversation with the past simple form of the verbs in brackets. Use auxiliary verbs and pronouns where necessary.**

Sam: Hi Joe! When ¹___did you get___ (get) back?
Joe: Yesterday afternoon.
Sam: Who ²_____ (go) on the school exchange?
Joe: Everyone in my class.
Sam: What ³_____ (happen) when you arrived?
Joe: We went to meet our families.
Sam: Who ⁴_____ (stay) with?
Joe: I stayed with a boy called Jean.
Sam: What kind of food ⁵_____ (eat)?
Joe: Lots of home cooking – Jean's dad's a great cook.
Sam: What ⁶_____ (do) there?
Joe: We went on trips and had lessons.
Sam: What trip ⁷_____ (like) best?
Joe: The riverboat trip.
Sam: Who ⁸_____ (speak) the best French now?
Joe: Well, I don't know. I learned a lot so maybe it's me!

Starter Unit

Adventure sports and activities

14 ★ Use the clues to complete the crossword.

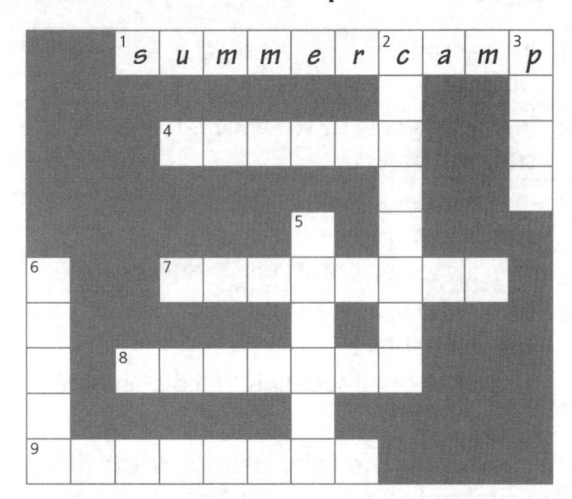

1 across: summer camp

Across
1 Young people often go to this in July or August. (2 words)
4 Going on this is a good way to see wild animals.
7 You do this type of long walk in the mountains.
8 You need a boat and a good wind for this activity.
9 You do this kind of visit with another school.

Down
2 You do this in the mountains, or inside on a wall.
3 See 6 down.
5 You do this in snow, normally in the winter.
6 and 3 down A fun place with lots of rides and shows. (2 words)

Present perfect with *ever*, *never*, *for* and *since*

15 ★ Complete the sentences with *ever*, *never*, *for* or *since*.
1 We've lived in this flat ___for___ eight years.
2 I've _____ been to summer camp, but I'd like to go one day.
3 She's studied ballet _____ 2009.
4 Have you _____ seen a shooting star?
5 That film's been on at the cinema _____ weeks. It's really popular.
6 We've been best friends _____ we started primary school.
7 They've _____ come to visit us here. We always go there.
8 Has he _____ met any famous actors?

Present perfect questions

16 ★★ Write present perfect questions for these answers.
1 *How long have you had your phone?*
 I've had my phone for a year.
2 _____
 No, I've never met a famous person.
3 _____
 We've lived in this flat since I was a baby.
4 _____
 Yes, I visited this gallery last year with my mum.
5 _____
 No, she hasn't been here for a long time.
6 _____
 He started playing the guitar when he was twelve.

Survival essentials

17 ★ Complete the words.

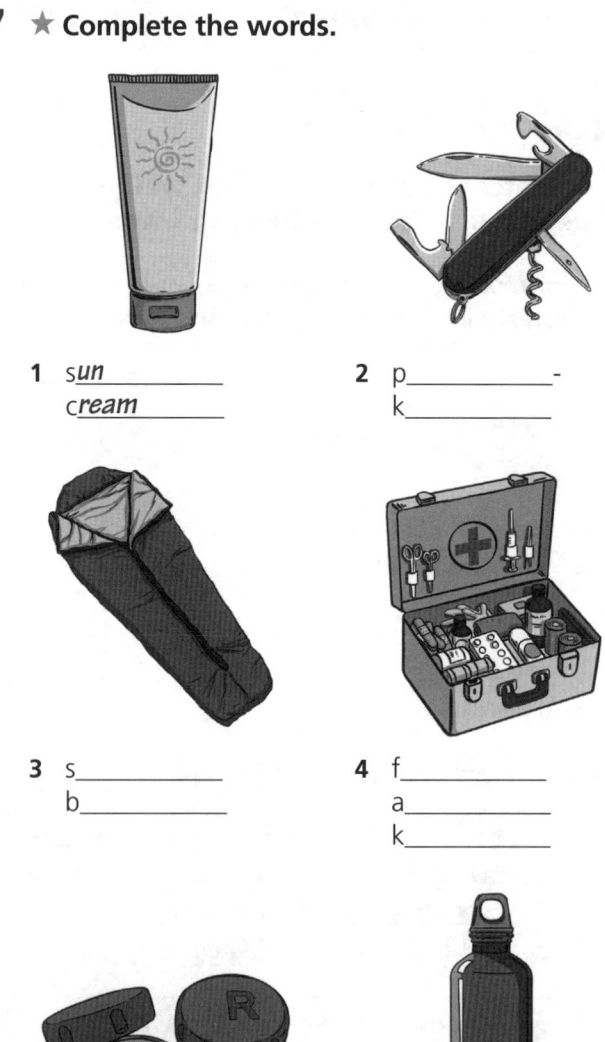

1 s*un*_____
 c*ream*_____

2 p_____-
 k_____

3 s_____
 b_____

4 f_____
 a_____
 k_____

5 c_____
 l_____

6 w_____
 b_____

6 Starter Unit

1 Trends

Vocabulary
Clothes

1 ★ Write the words for the clothes.

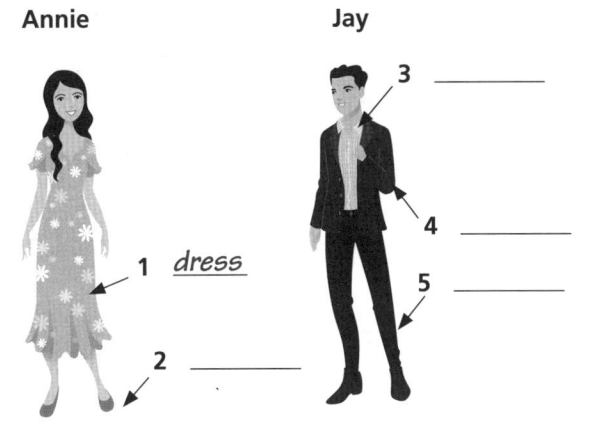

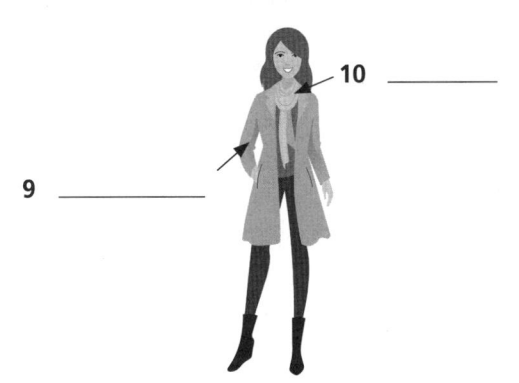

Annie
1 _dress_
2 _____

Jay
3 _____
4 _____
5 _____

Alexis
6 _____
7 _____

Leo
8 _____

Nicola
9 _____
10 _____

2 ★ Put the letters in order to make ten words to describe clothes.

1 tfal   _flat_
2 tpisyr   _____
3 dteift   _____
4 aeehlrt   _____
5 gygab   _____
6 ikls   _____
7 oloc   _____
8 wylfreo   _____
9 nedmi   _____
10 ghitt   _____

3 ★★ Look at the pictures in Exercise 1 again. Complete the descriptions with words from Exercise 2 and the people's names.

1 ___Jay___ 's wearing a ___leather___ jacket, a _____ shirt and _____ jeans.
2 _____ 's wearing a _____ dress and _____ shoes.
3 _____ 's wearing a _____ jumper.
4 _____ 's wearing a _____ coat and a _____ scarf.
5 _____ 's wearing a _____ skirt and a _____ T-shirt.

4 ★★ Complete the conversation with words from Exercises 1 and 2.

Nic: Hi Zac, have you been shopping?
Zac: Yes. Tell me what you think. Look at this denim ¹___jacket___. It's the latest fashion. I got a bigger size because I like ²_____ clothes, not fitted ones.
Nic: It's really cool! What else?
Zac: I got two warm wool ³_____ for the winter. This plain blue one, and this ⁴_____ one, I really like the red and green together.
Nic: Wow! It's very bright!
Zac: It's OK, it's not for school! What do you think of these? I needed some new ⁵_____ as my feet have grown, and these are real ⁶_____ , and black. I hope they're comfortable. I prefer trainers but we can't wear them to school. It's crazy!
Nic: They look alright. Is that all?
Zac: No, I also bought three white ⁷_____ for school, totally boring, I hate wearing a uniform and a tie! And finally, a pair of black denim ⁸_____ for the weekends, when I don't have to wear trousers.

5 ★★★ Write about your favourite clothes and what you usually wear. Write at least five sentences. Use vocabulary from Exercises 1 and 2.

My favourite clothes at the moment are my new tight black jeans and a T-shirt I bought on holiday.

Language focus 1

used to and *would*

1 ★ **Complete the rules in the table.**

1	We use *used to* and *would* to talk about past _____ .
2	After both *used to* and *would* we use the _____ form.
3	We use *did(n't)* in negative and question forms with _____ .
4	We only use *would* with _____ , like *play* or *go*. We use *used to* with actions and _____ verbs, like *be* or *have*.

2 ★ **Complete the sentences with the correct form of *used to* and the verbs in brackets.**

1. In the 1980s, most teenagers _____*used to talk*_____ (talk) for hours on the home phone.
2. When you were younger, _____ (have) long hair?
3. Every month, she _____ (spend) all her pocket money, but now she saves some.
4. When my granddad went to concerts in the 1960s, people _____ (sit) on the floor!
5. Fifty years ago, young people _____ (not listen) to music on the Internet.
6. I think my uncle _____ (be) a New Romantic!
7. Did your parents _____ (like) pop music when they were teenagers?
8. When I was little, my mum _____ (buy) all my clothes. I hated them!

3 ★ **Which five sentences from Exercise 2 can also be written with *would*? Rewrite the sentences here.**

1 In the 1980s, most teenagers would talk for hours on the home phone.
_____
_____
_____
_____
_____
_____

4 ★★ **Circle the correct options. If they are both correct, circle both.**

A: What's that photo?
B: It's my dad! He ¹(used to be)/ would be in a punk band and they ²used to travel / would travel all over the country to play concerts every weekend. He ³used to have / would have an old van to travel around in.
A: ⁴Did your mum use to be / Would your mum be a punk, too?
B: Well, sort of. She was a punk rock fan who ⁵used to go / would go to lots of local concerts and she wore punk clothes, but she ⁶didn't use to have / wouldn't have a punk hairstyle because she was still at school and her parents were strict.
A: What about your dad's hair?
B: Well, look at the photo! His hair's dyed bright green and yellow. Apparently he and his friends ⁷used to do / would do it themselves. Dad met Mum at a concert, but until he changed his hairstyle he ⁸didn't use to go / wouldn't go round to her house because she was worried about what her parents might say!
A: I can't believe that's your dad. He ⁹used to look / would look so different! I think I'll go home and ask my parents what they ¹⁰used to look like / would look like when they were teenagers!

5 ★★★ **Change these sentences so they are true for you.**

1. When I was younger, I would play pirates with my friends in the park.
_____
2. I used to wear make-up at birthday parties.
_____
3. I would choose my own clothes when I was younger.
_____
4. At primary school, we used to do lots of homework.
_____

We wouldn't play pirates in the park. We would play superheroes or football.

Listening and vocabulary

Listening

1 ★ 🔊 **01** Listen to a radio programme about school uniforms. Is the presenter for or against them?

2 ★★ 🔊 **01** Listen again and complete the presenter's notes.

Introduction:
Young people have ¹ __strong__ feelings about uniforms.
² _____ countries have them,
³ _____ countries don't.
In ⁴ _____ there was a big discussion about uniforms.

In favour:
Pupils feel ⁵ _____ of their school; all pupils look the ⁶ _____ ; they can concentrate on ⁷ _____ , not fashion.

Against:
Uniforms are ⁸ _____ and uncomfortable; students ⁹ _____ very quickly; teachers can't concentrate on ¹⁰ _____ ; uniforms aren't ¹¹ _____ for some subjects; uniforms don't help ¹² _____ or behaviour.

Uniforms today:
Girls can wear ¹³ _____ ; no shirts and ties is ¹⁴ _____ .

Discussion:
You can ¹⁵ _____ or email.

Adjectives and dependent prepositions

3 ★ Match the sentence beginnings (1–8) with the sentence endings (a–h).

1 My sister is so **afraid** __c__
2 I'm really **disappointed** ___
3 You must be **excited** ___
4 Why are you so **fascinated** ___
5 We're really **happy** ___
6 Is anyone **interested** ___
7 I'm not very **keen** ___
8 She's very **proud** ___

a **with** the clothes we bought yesterday.
b **on** heavy metal, it's too loud.
c **of** insects that she hates going in the garden.
d **of** her dress – she made it herself.
e **in** going to the sales with me on Saturday?
f **by** their new album. It's awful!
g **about** going to the concert next week.
h **by** the lives of celebrities?

4 ★★ Complete the text with the adjectives and prepositions from Exercise 3.

My cousins Andrea and Dani are really different. Dani's ¹ __fascinated by__ animals and has several pets, including a python. No one in his family is very ² _____ the situation, although he says being ³ _____ his snake is silly because it doesn't bite! Andrea's very ⁴ _____ music, and she plays the guitar in a new pop band. Their first concert is in ten days and they're really ⁵ _____ it, but Andrea is secretly a bit nervous! Dani isn't ⁶ _____ music at all – I don't think he ever listens to it – but he's really ⁷ _____ his sister's talent, and he wants us all to go to the concert together. I heard the band practising last week and I certainly wasn't ⁸ _____ their performance – they're really good!

Language focus 2

Past perfect

1 ★ (Circle) the correct words in the table.

1	We form the past perfect with *have* / *had* and the past participle.
2	We use the past perfect to talk about an action that happened **before** / **after** another action.
3	To talk about the most recent of two past actions, we use the **past simple** / **past perfect**.

2 ★ Complete the sentences with the past perfect form of the verbs in brackets.
1. Before Gianni went to college, he ___had designed___ (design) clothes for his friends.
2. We _____ (not be) at the shops long but we were really bored.
3. _____ (they/change) the uniform before you left school?
4. She _____ (not make) a dress before but it was quite easy.
5. Anna went back when she realised she _____ (leave) her leather jacket at home.
6. When you won the talent show, _____ (you/play) together in any other competitions?

3 ★★ (Circle) the correct options in the text.
When my next-door neighbour Alex ¹(came)/ had come back from his first term at university, he ²changed / had changed completely. He ³grew / had grown his hair long, and, when I saw him, he was wearing baggy cotton clothes instead of the cool clothes he ⁴wore / had worn before. He ⁵looked / had looked like a hippy! When I asked him about his new look, he told me that he ⁶went / had been to a meeting about the environment when he ⁷arrived / had arrived at university, and after a few weeks he ⁸joined / had joined Greenpeace. Now he says he's an eco-activist!

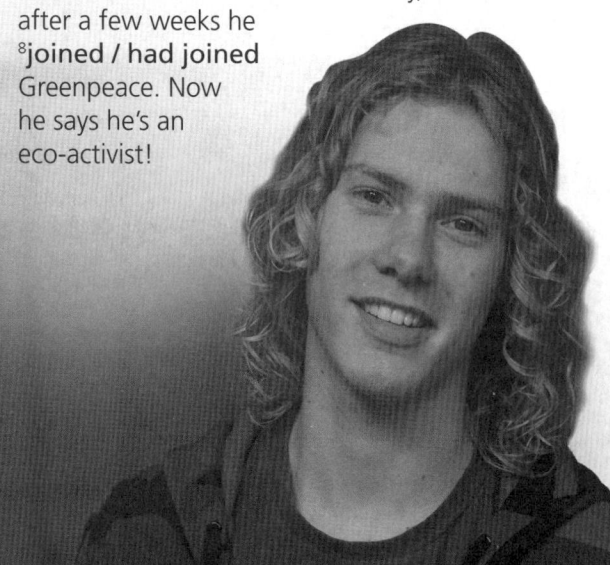

4 ★★ Complete the story with the past simple or past perfect form of the verbs in brackets.
I ¹___saw___ (see) a really nice jumper in town last week, but I ²_____ (not have) enough money with me. So I ³_____ (go) back to the shop on Saturday, but they ⁴_____ (sell) it. I ⁵_____ (feel) really disappointed. But when I ⁶_____ (get) home, my mum ⁷_____ (have) a surprise for me. It ⁸_____ (be) the same jumper! Although I ⁹_____ (not say) anything to her, she ¹⁰_____ (see) it in the shop window and ¹¹_____ (buy) it for me.

5 ★★★ Complete the sentences with the past perfect and your own ideas.
1. My friend finally arrived after _____ _____.
2. The concert was terrible although we _____ _____.
3. He was very excited about going to the fashion show because he _____ _____.
4. She wasn't very good at the new video game because _____.
5. I didn't go shopping because I _____ _____.

My friend finally arrived after I had waited for half an hour.

Explore compound nouns

6 ★★ Complete the sentences with a word from box A followed by a word from box B.

A | ~~style~~   motor   taxi   guitar   telephone   street

B | music   ~~consultant~~   art   box   industry   driver

1. Famous people often employ a ___style consultant___ to help them decide what clothes to wear.
2. In many big cities today there is a lot of _____ – some of it can be really beautiful, but not always!
3. We went to a concert of classical _____ last night. I wasn't expecting to enjoy it, but it was really relaxing.
4. Everyone in my family works in the _____ – my brother is a mechanic, my dad works in a factory and my mum designs new models.
5. I didn't have my mobile with me yesterday, so I was looking for a _____ , but of course I couldn't find one.
6. I don't think I'd like to work as a _____ because I hate sitting in traffic jams.

Reading

1 ★ Read the article about Comic-Con. Tick (✓) the kind of people who go there.

famous actors ☐   young people ☐
comic artists ☐   teachers ☐
young children ☐ science-fiction writers ☐

GEEKS AND SUPERHEROES

Do you like comics? In the 1950s and 60s, many teenagers used to read comics like Batman, Superman or X Men. Some were so fascinated by comics that they would continue reading them when they grew up. They were comic '**geeks**': intelligent, often unsociable young people who identified more with the worlds of fantasy and science fiction than the real world. Geeks still exist today; in the popular TV comedy series *The Big Bang Theory*, the main characters are science geeks who are big fans of comics, fantasy games and Comic-Con.

Comic-Con doesn't try to make money. In fact it describes itself as a **non-profit organisation** that exists to make comics and related art forms more popular through conventions and events. In 1970, a group of about 100 comic fans got together in San Diego, California for the first Comic-Con, or convention. They decided to include not only comics, but also other aspects of popular culture, including fantasy and science-fiction games, books and films from all over the world. Within 30 years, Comic-Con had grown into a huge three-day international convention, with over 120,000 visitors every year. Today there are exhibitions, comics to buy, games to play, educational sessions, talks, a film festival, and even an **awards** ceremony known as the 'Oscars' of the comic industry.

Nowadays, there are comic conventions all over the world, but Comic-Con is the most iconic. It attracts famous film stars, writers and artists from the world of comics. Many of the fans who visit it wear costumes of comic book characters, and sometimes famous stars wear a **disguise** too so they can **wander round** the convention like all the other fans. In 2014, Daniel Radcliffe walked around Comic-Con dressed in a Spiderman costume with a face mask, and no one recognised him. So if you go to Comic-Con, you never know who might be next to you!

2 ★★ Complete the sentences with the words in **bold** from the text.
1 He's a really good footballer and has won a lot of Player of the Year _____ .
2 My sister and her friends spend all their time on maths problems. They are such _____ !
3 We're going to _____ the old town this morning and look at the little shops.
4 I help at an animal rescue centre. It's a(n) _____ , so they don't pay me.
5 The pop star didn't want anyone to see him, so he went shopping in _____ .

3 ★★ Choose the correct answers.
1 What used to be popular with teenagers in the 1950s and 60s?
   a stories about superheroes
   b science-fiction and fantasy games
2 When was the first Comic-Con convention?
   a in the 1950s   b in 1970
3 What can you see at Comic-Con today?
   a lots of different things
   b comics, games, books and TV comedy programmes
4 How can famous people become 'invisible' at Comic-Con?
   a by behaving like all the other fans
   b by wearing a disguise

4 ★★ Read the article again. Who or what is each sentence about?
1 Teenagers started reading them in the 1950s and 60s.   *comics*
2 They preferred a fantasy world to real life.   _____
3 Its aim is to make the worlds of fantasy and science fiction better known.   _____
4 The 100 people who met in San Diego in 1970 for the first convention.   _____
5 This is what Comic-Con has become.   _____
6 There are more than a hundred thousand of these.   _____
7 You can learn and get information about the world of comics at these.   _____
8 Definitely the most famous comic event internationally.   _____
9 Many of the visitors wear these at Comic-Con.   _____
10 He visited Comic-Con and no one knew who he was.   _____

5 ★★★ Do you sometimes read comics? Which ones? Would you like to go to Comic-Con? Why/Why not? Would you wear a costume? Who would you dress as?

Writing

A biography

1 Read the biography of The Beach Boys. How long have the band been together?

The Beach Boys formed in California in 1961. The original members were Brian Wilson, his two brothers, Dennis and Carl, his cousin Mike Love and a friend, Al Jardine. ¹ _Although_ the group started around the same time as surfing became much more popular in California, the only member of the band who used to surf was Dennis.

² _____ releasing their first album, *Surfin' Safari*, there was a huge rise in the popularity of surf culture on the west coast of the USA. The band had their biggest international hit with their most famous album, *Pet Sounds*, and the single *Good Vibrations*. ³ _____ that time, they were the only American band who could compete with The Beatles and most people think that they are one of America's greatest rock bands.

⁴ _____ the years, 36 of their songs have been in the US Top 40 and ⁵ _____ a result they have sold over 100 million records around the world. Incredibly, the band is still playing – with some different members – and ⁶ _____ the last few years they have continued to tour.

2 Read the biography again. Complete the sentences.
1. The Beach Boys originally had ___five___ members in the band.
2. They started playing music together in _____ , USA.
3. The band were popular at the same time as _____ culture in the USA.
4. Their most successful single was _____ .
5. They've had _____ songs in the Top 40.
6. The band still play together and _____ .

Useful language Sequencers and connectors

3 Complete the biography with the words in the box.

| as   After   Over   ~~Although~~   in   During |

4 Circle the correct words.
1. After / **In** the last few years, their music has become more popular.
2. Although / As they came from the UK, they were also very popular in the USA.
3. They were very famous in the 1990s and **over / during** that time they played a lot of concerts.
4. They formed in 2001 and **in / over** the next 10 years became the biggest band in the world.
5. Although / After having three number 1 singles in a row, she began to work with other bands.
6. Jack started a solo career and **as / in** a result the band split up in 2013.

WRITING TIP

Make it better! ✓✓✓
Use *one of* and a superlative adjective to say that what you are talking about is very special in some way.
The Beatles are **one of the most famous** pop groups ever.

Writing

5 Complete the sentences with *one of* and the correct form of the adjectives in brackets.
1. Nirvana were <u>one of the most successful</u> (successful) bands to come out of Seattle.
2. In the 1990s, U2 were _____ (big) touring bands in the world.
3. Green Day have always been _____ (popular) punk bands in the USA.
4. Beyoncé is _____ (rich) female singers nowadays.
5. For a while, Eminem was _____ (interesting) rap artists in the world.

6 Put the words in brackets in the correct place in the sentences.
1. She had a number 1 hit in 2012 with *Firework*. (again)
   <u>She had a number 1 hit again in 2012 with Firework.</u>
2. He has sold over 20 million copies of his latest album. (now)
3. They are touring today after 30 years. (still)
4. She sang many of her songs in French. (also)
5. They were one of the most successful bands. (ever)

> **WRITING TIP**
> Make it better! ✓ ✓ ✓
> Talk about the influence or impact the band or artist has had on the present.
> *Elvis Presley died in 1977, but everyone still recognises his music even today.*

7 Read the sentences. Which one does <u>not</u> talk about the present?
1. Their music lives on long after they split up.
2. Her music has become popular with the release of the film.
3. The band's music is still popular today even after 40 years.
4. He was never as successful in his own country as in the USA.
5. She is still touring today and singing the songs everyone loves.

8 Read the biography in Exercise 1 again and tick (✓) the information it includes.
- information about the members of the band ✓
- their recent work ☐
- the number of number 1 hits ☐
- some of their most famous lyrics ☐
- the number of records they have sold ☐
- problems the band had in their career ☐
- when and where they formed ☐
- the name of a well-known album or single ☐
- the names of bands that they have influenced ☐

PLAN

9 Think of a famous band or artist who started a long time ago but is still successful today. Find out more information about them. Then use the categories in Exercise 8 and make notes.

WRITE

10 Write a biography of the band or artist. Look at page 17 of the Student's Book to help you.

_____

CHECK

11 Check your writing. Can you say YES to these questions?
- Have you used the ideas in Exercise 8?
- Have you used sequencers to order your ideas?
- Have you used connectors to join your ideas?
- Have you used superlatives correctly?
- Have you put the words in the correct order?
- Have you talked about the band or artist's influence or impact on the present?
- Are the spelling and punctuation correct?

Do you need to write a second draft?

1 Review

Vocabulary
Clothes

1 Match the words in the box with the clothes in the pictures. Write the adjectives and the clothes together. There are four extra words.

> denim fitted flat leather silk
> stripy tight flowery baggy cool

1 _a fitted coat_
2 _____ 
3 _____ 
4 _____ 
5 _____ 
6 _____ 

Total: 5

Adjectives and dependent prepositions

2 Complete the sentences with the correct preposition.
1 Is everyone happy __with__ spaghetti for supper?
2 My little brother is afraid _____ dogs.
3 She was disappointed _____ her birthday present.
4 My mum says she's proud _____ all her children.
5 He's fascinated _____ insects.
6 Are you excited _____ moving to Australia?
7 I'm not keen _____ the idea of living abroad.
8 I'm not very interested _____ fashion, it's boring.

Total: 7

Language focus
used to and would

3 Complete the conversation with the correct form of *used to* or *would* and the verbs in brackets. If both are possible, use *would*.

A: My dad ¹ __used to be__ (be) a professional tennis player. He and his coach ² _____ (travel) all over the world, and we ³ _____ (not see) him for weeks or months.
B: ⁴ _____ (your mum/be) with you at home?
A: Yes, she ⁵ _____ (not like) leaving us, but of course she ⁶ _____ (attend) important matches.
B: ⁷ _____ (you/go) to any matches?
A: No, not often, because I ⁸ _____ (have) school, but in the holidays, yes. Then we ⁹ _____ (stay) in big hotels and we ¹⁰ _____ (love) it!

Total: 9

Past perfect

4 Write sentences with the prompts. Use the past simple and the past perfect in each sentence.
1 The town / change / a lot / when / she / go back / for a visit
   The town had changed a lot when she went back for a visit.
2 I / not see / Melanie / in a dress / before / she / wear / one / to the party
   _____
3 After / he / buy / the shoes / he / go / home
   _____
4 We / not be / there / long / when / it / start / to rain
   _____
5 They / decide / to wait / until / they / finish / their homework
   _____
6 the concert / start / when / you / get / there?
   _____

Total: 5

14 Unit 1

Language builder

5 (Circle) the correct options.
1. How / **What** was your holiday like?
2. Who **did make** / **made** this terrible mess? Tidy it up now!
3. He's **just** / **still** finished practising the guitar, but he **just** / **still** hasn't done any homework.
4. She's **ever** / **never** been sailing before.
5. We've lived here **since** / **for** my sister was born.
6. While they **were trekking** / **trekked** in the Rockies, he **was falling** / **fell** and **was breaking** / **broke** his ankle.
7. I haven't made that phone call **yet** / **already**. I keep forgetting.
8. When **does start the new school year** / **does the new school year start**?
9. **Did you use to** / **Would you** have long hair when you were a teenager, Dad?
10. When we moved to this village, I **lived** / **had lived** in four different places already.
11. A: **Have you been** / **Did you go** on a safari before?
    B: Yes, I **'ve been** / **went** on one two years ago. It **'s been** / **was** lots of fun.

Total: 15

Vocabulary builder

6 (Circle) the correct options.
1. When they heard the scream, they were all ___ .
   a exciting   **b terrified**   c worrying
2. It's really important to take a ___ on a walk just in case of accidents.
   a first aid kit   b pen-knife   c sun cream
3. We decided to ___ really early in the morning because it was a long journey.
   a look round   b chill out   c set off
4. I would never go ___ because I'm afraid of heights.
   a sailing   b climbing   c theme park
5. Don't forget to ___ the lights. We're trying to save electricity.
   a turn down   b reduce   c switch off
6. I really like the new ___ in the middle of the square outside the art gallery.
   a sculpture   b portrait   c mural
7. It wasn't difficult to ___ new friends when I moved to my new school.
   a make   b know   c do
8. That's a really pretty ___ . Are you wearing it to the wedding?
   a flat shoes   b tight jeans   c flowery dress
9. That walk yesterday was great but really ___ . I went to bed early.
   a interested   b tiring   c boring
10. How can you ___ so much electricity? Be more careful!
    a save   b waste   c leave on
11. Are you interested ___ joining the gym?
    a on   b about   c in

Total: 10

Speaking

7 Complete the conversation with the phrases in the box.

> don't fit   look great   ~~my size~~
> suits you   the changing rooms
> these shoes

Nik: I need a dress and some shoes for the party. Let's have a look.
Amy: Do you like this dress?
Nik: Oh, yes, it's really pretty, and it's ¹_____my size_____ , too.
Amy: How about ²_____ ? They're perfect for a party.
Nik: Wow, yes. OK, I need to try everything on. Where are ³_____ ?
Amy: I think they're on the left at the back. Come on.
…
Nik: So, what do you think?
Amy: Oh the dress really ⁴_____ . And the shoes ⁵_____ , too!
Nik: Yes, but they ⁶_____ very well! They're a bit tight.
Amy: That's a pity. Well, just buy the dress then. There's a fantastic shoe shop near here. We can go there next.

Total: 5

Total: 56

Unit 1   15

Get it right! Unit 1

used to or use to?

Remember that:
- we use **used to** + infinitive to talk about past habits and states in affirmative sentences.
  - ✓ Punks **used to wear** dog collars as necklaces.
  - ✗ Punks ~~use to~~ wear dog collars as necklaces.
- we use **did(n't)** + subject + **use to** without the 'd' in questions.
  - ✓ **Did you use to** walk to school on your own?
  - ✗ ~~Did you used to~~ walk to school on your own?
- we use **did(n't)** + **use to** without the 'd' in negative sentences.
  - ✓ They **didn't use to** spend a lot of money on clothes.
  - ✗ They ~~didn't used to~~ spend a lot of money on clothes.

1 Complete the sentences with *used to* or *use to*.
1. My mum __used to__ wear flowery dresses.
2. They didn't _____ wear a uniform.
3. Did you _____ be friends with Marco?
4. We _____ go to the same school.
5. She _____ come to my house on Saturdays.
6. How often did you _____ read fashion magazines?
7. I didn't _____ like him, but now we're good friends.
8. My brother _____ have long hair and wear make-up.

Past perfect

Remember that:
- we use **had** + past participle to form the past perfect. Don't forget to use **had**!
  - ✓ I **had never been** to a live concert before the concert last week.
  - ✗ ~~I never been~~ to a live concert before the concert last week.
- we use the **past perfect** to talk about an action that happened **before** another action. We use the **past simple** to talk about the **most recent** of two actions.
  - ✓ When I **arrived**, Joe **had already gone** home.
  - ✗ When I arrived, ~~Joe already went~~ home.
  - ✗ When I ~~had~~ arrived, Joe had already gone home.

2 Are the sentences correct? Correct the incorrect sentences.
1. Rory never been camping before. He loved it!
   Rory had never been camping before. He loved it!
2. She had just started to do her homework when the phone rang.
   _____
3. Sarah saw that Julian forgot his keys.
   _____
4. We had to walk to school because our dad was sold the car.
   _____
5. She was happy because she always wanted to meet him.
   _____
6. They arrived at the concert late because they had got lost.
   _____
7. They ate all the pizza before we had arrived.
   _____
8. The dog was afraid because it was heard fireworks.
   _____

Clothes

Remember that:
- **clothes** are things like dresses and trousers that cover our body. A **cloth** is a piece of material we use for cleaning things. Don't confuse *clothes* and *cloth*.
  - ✓ I've just bought some new **clothes**.
  - ✗ I've just bought some new ~~cloths~~.
  - ✓ Clean the glasses with a soft **cloth**.
- **clothes** is always plural. It does not have a singular form without *-s* and we do not say 'a clothe' or 'a clothes'.
  - ✓ I like having new **clothes** to wear.
  - ✗ I like having ~~a new clothe~~ to wear.
- we use the verb **wear** to talk about having some clothes on our body. Don't say *use*.
  - ✓ I like **wearing** shorts in the summer.
  - ✗ I like ~~using~~ shorts in the summer.

3 Find and correct five more mistakes in these sentences.
1. I love ~~using~~ *wearing* jeans! They're so comfortable.
2. I bought a dress from the new cloth shop in my town.
3. I'm not interested in clothe and I don't like shopping.
4. I don't spend a lot of money on clothes.
5. You should use old clothes because we're going to paint my bedroom.
6. What kind of clothes do you like wearing?
7. My sister always wears a fashionable clothes.
8. People usually wear traditional cloths for weddings.

2 A helping hand

Vocabulary
Personal qualities

1 ★ **Find nine more personal qualities in the wordsquare.**

i	e	a	s	y	g	o	i	n	g	h	t
m	p	r	e	d	s	u	b	a	n	a	a
p	a	l	s	e	t	y	p	e	i	r	l
a	s	m	o	t	i	v	a	t	e	d	s
t	s	r	w	e	a	s	h	c	i	w	o
i	i	o	n	r	s	h	y	s	t	o	c
e	o	p	v	m	s	e	n	t	e	r	i
n	n	s	a	i	v	a	r	m	k	a	
t	a	l	e	n	t	e	d	i	r	i	b
n	t	u	s	e	a	w	o	c	i	n	l
d	e	d	y	d	r	i	c	t	y	g	e

2 ★ **Complete the definitions with the words in Exercise 1.**
1 When you really want to do something, you're _motivated_ .
2 When you want everything to happen quickly, you're _____ .
3 When you have a special ability for something, you're _____ .
4 When you're relaxed about everything, you're _____ .
5 When you make sure that rules are never broken, you're _____ .
6 When you like meeting people, you're _____ .
7 When you work a lot, you're _____ .
8 When you're not confident around people, you're _____ .
9 When you have strong feelings about something, you're _____ about it.
10 When you never give up, you're _____ .

3 ★★ **Complete the sentences with words from Exercise 1.**
1 Our History teacher is great. She's really _passionate_ about history and she makes it real.
2 I think you're really _____ . Why don't you enter the competition? I'm sure you can win!
3 His parents are quite _____ and are never angry when he gets home late.
4 He's so _____ . He studies for hours every day, doing the homework and then extra!
5 Athletes need to be very _____ to go out training when it's cold and wet.
6 I don't mind waiting five minutes in a shop, but I get _____ if I have to wait for a long time.

4 ★★ **Complete the text with personal qualities.**
Laura, one of the girls in my class, is very ¹ _shy_ . She doesn't usually say much and, because she isn't very ² _____ , she hasn't got a lot of friends. So everyone was surprised when she got a big part in the school play. We soon discovered why though, she's really ³ _____ about acting, and a different person on stage. The drama teacher, Mrs Martin, is quite ⁴ _____ and most people are scared of her. If you can't remember your words, she can be quite ⁵ _____ , and gets angry very quickly! Laura, though, is very ⁶ _____ . She learned her part quickly and did extra practice, so Mrs Martin was very pleased. Laura was amazing in the play – she's so ⁷ _____ , the best actress in the school! Now she says she wants to be a professional actress when she leaves school, and Mrs Martin is helping her. She seems really ⁸ _____ .

5 ★★★ **Which of the adjectives describe you? Why? Write at least five sentences.**

I'm very determined. Learning to skateboard was difficult but I did it!

Unit 2 17

Language focus 1

Reflexive pronouns and *each other*

1 ★ **Complete the tables with reflexive pronouns.**

Singular

I	you	he	she	it
		himself		

Plural

we	you	they

2 ★ **Complete the sentences with the correct reflexive pronoun.**
1. I'm making __myself__ a sandwich.
2. Karen cut _____ on some broken glass on the beach.
3. We really enjoyed _____ at the party. Thanks!
4. They bought _____ some new clothes in the sales.
5. My computer turns _____ off to save energy when I don't use it.
6. Here's the pizza, everyone! You can all help _____ .
7. He hurt _____ quite badly when he fell off his bike.
8. Wow! Did you do that all by _____ or did someone else help you?

3 ★ **Complete the sentences in the table.**

1	When John looks at John in the mirror, we say he looks at _____ .
2	When Annie texts Kate and Kate texts Annie, we say they text _____ .

4 ★★ (Circle) **the correct words.**
1. My friends and I always help **ourselves /** (**each other**) when we have a problem.
2. Did you enjoy **yourselves / each other** at the amusement park?
3. Harry taught **himself / each other** to play the guitar.
4. My best friend and I text **ourselves / each other** a lot when we go on holiday.
5. Luckily, Paula didn't hurt **herself / each other** when she fell off her bike.
6. They go to different schools but they see **themselves / each other** at the weekend.

5 ★★ **Complete the postcard with reflexive pronouns and *each other*.**

Dear Mum and Dad,
Are you enjoying ¹ __yourselves__ without us?! It was a bit boring here with Granny and Granddad at first. There's no Internet, so we had to find ² _____ things to do. Joey has taught ³ _____ to skateboard, and I'm making ⁴ _____ a jumper for the winter – Granny's showing me how. Nice surprise though – I saw Marie yesterday! We hadn't seen ⁵ _____ since we were little. We spent ages telling ⁶ _____ all our news – I was late for supper! Her parents have built ⁷ _____ a house here, so we can entertain ⁸ _____ all summer.
See you soon!
Love
Patri

6 ★★★ **Write answers to the questions.**
1. How do you and your friends enjoy yourselves?
   _____
2. Did you teach yourself to read?
   _____
3. When do your family give each other presents?
   _____
4. What do your friends do to stop themselves getting bored?
   _____
5. What do you and your classmates help each other with?
   _____

We enjoy ourselves by playing video games.

Explore word building

7 ★★ **Complete the second sentence with the related adjective or noun.**
1. She's very **determined**.
   She's got a lot of __determination__ .
2. He sings with so much **passion**!
   He's really _____ about singing.
3. To be a gymnast, you need to be **flexible**.
   You need a lot of _____ to be a gymnast.
4. Going on holiday makes me **happy**.
   My idea of _____ is going on holiday.
5. Climbing that mountain is quite a **challenge**.
   That mountain is quite _____ to climb.
6. His first album was an immediate **success**.
   His first album was immediately _____ .

18 Unit 2

Listening and vocabulary

Listening

1 ★ 🔊 02 **Listen to an interview with a sprinter called Errol Dixon. Why is he unusual?**
  a He is blind.
  b He runs a lot of races.
  c He races with another runner.

2 ★★ 🔊 02 **Listen again and choose the correct options.**
  1 A guide runner …
    (a) helps a blind runner in races.
    b only runs with other sprinters.
  2 Liz Stevens …
    a was born blind.
    b runs at more than one distance.
  3 The most important thing for a guide runner is …
    a helping the other runner in training.
    b moving their arms and legs with the other runner.
  4 Errol and Liz …
    a are joined together in a race.
    b don't need to think when they race.
  5 Errol and Liz talk …
    a at the beginning of the race.
    b during every race.
  6 Errol became a guide runner …
    a through a family member.
    b after he was in the Olympics in Beijing.
  7 Errol and Liz …
    a have been together since they met in Beijing.
    b want to compete in the Paralympics.
  8 Errol explains that he and Liz …
    a won a gold medal at London 2012.
    b both get a gold medal if they win.

Phrasal verbs (learning and socialising)

3 ★ **Complete the phrasal verbs with the prepositions in the box.**

| ~~up~~ up up up with together |
| on on on to |

  1 create something new — set __up__
  2 join a class or other organised activity — sign _____
  3 respect someone — look _____ _____
  4 teach or give new information — pass _____
  5 depend on someone — count _____
  6 have a good relationship with someone — get _____ _____
  7 stop doing something — give _____
  8 help people be friendly to each other — bring _____

4 ★★ **Complete the sentences with the phrasal verbs from Exercise 3.**
  1 If you need any help, just ask. You can always _count on_ me.
  2 My granny's teaching me to cook. She says it's important to _____ her skills.
  3 I really _____ my next-door neighbour. She's 72, but she's a good friend.
  4 They are planning to _____ a chess club at school this term. I wanted all my friends to _____ , but most of them weren't interested!
  5 Joey decided to _____ football, because all the training sessions were too much with schoolwork.
  6 We hope to _____ old and young people to help each other with this new project.
  7 Young people often _____ sports people or musicians.

Language focus 2

Present perfect simple

1 ★ (Circle) the correct words in the table.

1	We can use the present perfect simple to talk about a series of actions in the **past / present**.
2	We often use the present perfect simple to ask about **how many / how long**.

2 ★★ Write present perfect simple sentences with the prompts.

1 pieces of pizza / you / eat?
   <u>How many pieces of pizza have you eaten?</u>
2 She / win / a lot of competitions
   _____
3 We / make / three cakes for the party
   _____
4 times / they / go / there?
   _____
5 I / send / 100 texts / this week
   _____
6 people / he / invite / to the birthday party?
   _____

Present perfect continuous

3 ★ Complete the rules in the table.

1	We use the present perfect continuous to refer to a time period that _____ finished.
2	We often use the present perfect continuous to ask about how _____ .
3	We can use the present perfect continuous to refer to actions we expect to _____ in the future.

4 ★★ Complete the sentences with the present perfect continuous form of the verbs in the box.

look   run   practise   ~~come~~   go   work

1 My family ____<u>has been coming</u>____ to this campsite for ten years.
2 She _____ the piano every night for the concert.
3 We _____ on our project every weekend for weeks.
4 My parents _____ for a new car for weeks.
5 I _____ to the youth club for two months. It's great!
6 David _____ in races since he was 10.

Present perfect simple vs. present perfect continuous

5 ★★★ Your friend Callum does a lot of work with a charity. Answer the questions with full sentences using the words in brackets.

1 How many people have visited your charity's website this year, Callum? (about 100,000)
   <u>About 100,000 people have visited our website.</u>
2 How long have you been doing charity work? (every Saturday for two years)
   _____
3 What activities have you been doing this year to make money? (parachute jumps and quizzes)
   _____
4 How many parachute jumps have you organised? (four so far)
   _____
5 Who has the charity been helping this year? (groups of children all over the country)
   _____
6 How many children has the charity helped? (thousands)
   _____

6 ★★★ Write questions with the present perfect simple and continuous. Answer them for you.

1 How many / films / you / watch / this week?
   _____
2 How long / you / come / this school?
   _____
3 you / learn English / a long time?
   _____
4 How many times / you / look / your mobile phone / today?
   _____

How many films have you watched this week?
I haven't watched any!

Reading

1 ★ Read the article about Lady Gaga's charity. What is the charity's message?
   a 'Different is best'
   b 'Accept individual differences'
   c 'Singing is good for you'

BORN THIS WAY

Stefani Germanotta, better known as Lady Gaga, is famous for her extravagant style. She has always been different, and she says that's why she was bullied when she was at secondary school. Gaga has told the media that other pupils **made fun of** her for being ugly, being fat, having a big nose, being annoying, having a funny laugh and being **weird**. She was also constantly asked why she always sang, why she was so keen on theatre and why she did her make-up the way she did. Gaga has said that sometimes it got so bad she didn't even want to go to school.

Since then Lady Gaga has become rich, famous and successful for some of the things she was once bullied about, so she decided to try and help young people who found themselves in the situation she was in at school. In 2011, she and her mother Cynthia started a non-profit organisation called the Born This Way Foundation, (BTWF). Its aim is to build a society where people accept each other's differences and individuality. Gaga wants to bring young people together to create a new kind of community, based on three things: safety, and the skills and opportunities to make a kinder, braver world.

For many teenagers who are bullied, home is no escape because the **bullying** continues online. Lady Gaga has met Barack Obama to discuss action against cyber-bullying, and also demands more **moderators** on social media sites.

BTWF has been helping young people to set up 'Born Brave' school and community groups. The aim of these is to encourage young people to be more **tolerant**. The charity wants everyone to feel safe in their community, school, home, wherever they live, and to develop the skills they need to live in peace with other people.

2 ★★ Match the words in **bold** in the text with the definitions.
   1 accepting that people are different _____
   2 say horrible things about _____
   3 people who delete bad comments on social media sites _____
   4 being cruel to or hurting someone weaker _____
   5 strange or unusual _____

3 ★★ Read the first paragraph again. Complete the table with the reasons why Lady Gaga was bullied.

Appearance	Personality	Interests	Behaviour
ugly			

4 ★★★ Now read the rest of the article again. Complete the notes about the charity.

Name: [1] _the Born This Way Foundation_

Started: in [2] _____ by
[3] _____

Aim: [4] _____

Idea is: to create a community with
[5] _____, [6] _____ and [7] _____
to make the world better

Charity also wants: to stop [8] _____ bullying
on [9] _____ sites

'Born Brave' groups: work with [10] _____
people in their [11] _____ and [12] _____

5 ★★★ What do you think of Lady Gaga's charity? Is it necessary where you live? Why/Why not? Write at least five sentences.

Writing

A personal email

1 Read Olivia's email. Why is she writing to Sophie?

Dear Sophie,

I'm writing to say thank you for all the help you gave me when my family and I came to live in Dublin. Going to live in another city was very difficult and at the beginning I ¹ _found_ Dublin so strange compared to the neighbourhood where you and I lived in Liverpool. I also ² _____ really different from everyone here but your advice to sign up for lots of after-school activities really helped. I've been learning a bit of Irish, which I ³ _____ really confusing, and I'm learning to play the guitar. I'm determined to make more friends and to be more sociable.

Speaking to each other on Skype™ is great and all those amazing messages you've been sending me are really motivating. It's been great to be able to count on you when I'm ⁴ _____ lonely. I've made a few friends and now I'm ⁵ _____ life here much easier. I've been telling them all about you. I hope you come and visit soon.

Anyway, thanks again for everything. You're a great friend.

Lots of love,

Olivia

---

2 Read the email again. Answer the questions.
1. Where does Olivia live now?
   She lives in Dublin.
2. How does she know Sophie?
3. What advice did Sophie give Olivia?
4. What after-school activities is Olivia doing?
5. How do Olivia and Sophie contact each other?
6. How has Olivia's life changed since she followed Sophie's advice?

Useful language — Expressing how we feel

3 Complete Olivia's email with the correct form of *feel* or *find*.

4 Write sentences with *feel* or *find* and your own ideas.
1. learning English / difficult
   I find learning English very difficult.
2. shy / I first came to this school
3. Maths / difficult at the beginning
4. determined / get on with my new friends
5. meeting new people / hard
6. motivated / try new things

5 Rewrite the sentences using an *-ing* form at the beginning.
1. It wasn't as difficult to make new friends as I thought.
   Making new friends wasn't as difficult as I thought.
2. It is always easier for you to meet new people after school.
3. It was a wonderful experience to bring all my friends together.
4. It has been great fun to go to swimming classes with you.
5. I've been writing a diary and that's been very useful.

Writing

6 Circle the correct words.
1. At first, I felt really **bored** / boring all the time.
2. At the beginning, I found your advice really motivated / motivating.
3. I wasn't very worried / worrying about missing so many swimming lessons.
4. I've always found History very confused / confusing – so many dates!
5. I felt a bit depressed / depressing about moving to another city.
6. It's been really amazed / amazing to make new friends.

> **WRITING TIP**
> Make it better! ✓ ✓ ✓
> In your email, put in some sentences which talk directly to the person you are writing to.
> *You have helped me so much, you're the best friend I could wish for.*

7 Read the sentences. Which one does not talk directly to the reader?
1. You know how impatient I can be.
2. You've been such a great help to me over the last few months.
3. Getting these messages has been very important to me.
4. I always felt really determined after talking to you.
5. You're such an easy-going person and a really good friend.

8 Put the information in the order it appears in Olivia's email in Exercise 1.

> how she felt about the changes in her life
> why she's writing
> how her friend helped her
> say thank you
> what she's doing to solve her problems
> how her life has changed

1. *why she's writing*
2. _____
3. _____
4. _____
5. _____
6. _____

PLAN

9 You are going to write a thank you email to a friend or family member who gave you advice in a difficult situation. Choose one of the situations below. Use the categories in Exercise 8 and make notes.
- You were having a lot of trouble with a subject at school.
- You did an exchange with a student in another country.
- You were often bored after school.
- You were finding concentrating on your homework very difficult.

WRITE

10 Write your thank you email. Look at page 27 of the Student's Book to help you.

CHECK

11 Check your writing. Can you say YES to these questions?
- Have you used the ideas in Exercise 8?
- Have you used *feel* and *find* to express your feelings?
- Have you written a sentence with an *-ing* form at the beginning?
- Have you used *-ed* and *-ing* adjectives correctly?
- Have you used some sentences which talk directly to the reader?
- Are the spelling and punctuation correct?

Do you need to write a second draft?

2 Review

Vocabulary
Personal qualities

1 Match the sentences (1–6) with the sentences (a–f) that follow them.
1. My sister's so **impatient**. _b_
2. Janie's parents are quite **strict**. ___
3. I'm not feeling very **sociable** today. ___
4. She's really **motivated**. ___
5. She's too **easy-going**. ___
6. Your parents are very **hard-working**. ___

a I don't want to go to the party.
b She hates waiting, everything has to happen now!
c They both work long hours in the restaurant.
d She always does what other people want to do.
e They don't let her come out with us very often.
f She practises a lot more than the rest of us.

Total: 5

Phrasal verbs (learning and socialising)

2 (Circle) the correct phrasal verbs.
Many young people, especially boys, ¹(look up to) / get on with professional footballers. Some players use the relationship they have with their fans to help them ²pass on / give up anti-social behaviour, and find a job. They try to ³pass on / bring together their own life experiences and sometimes ⁴give up / set up their own charities to ⁵bring together / look up to boys and girls from different neighbourhoods. These young people can ⁶count on / sign up for sports activities, educational courses or job training.

Total: 5

Language focus
Reflexive pronouns and *each other*

3 Complete the conversations with reflexive pronouns or *each other*.

Nina: Great party, Sue. Everyone's enjoying ¹ _themselves_ !
Sue: Thanks! Hey guys! There's lots of food in the kitchen. Just help ² _____ !

Jake: Did you teach ³ _____ to play the guitar? I tried to teach ⁴ _____ once, but I couldn't do it!
Kim: Well, Gary was teaching ⁵ _____ at the same time, so we helped ⁶ _____ .

Total: 5

Present perfect simple

4 Write present perfect simple sentences.
1. We / learn / a lot of things / in Biology / this term
   We've learned a lot of things in Biology this term.
2. How many / text messages / you / send / today?
   _____
3. They / win / several awards / for their charity work
   _____
4. I / not have / any exams / this month
   _____
5. How many / times / she / go / to the youth club?
   _____
6. He / help / a lot of people / with problems
   _____

Total: 5

Present perfect continuous

5 Complete the sentences with the present perfect continuous form of the verbs in the box.

give   not go   come   help   ~~visit~~   make

1. You _'ve been visiting_ him a lot recently.
2. How long _____ you _____ to class?
3. She _____ to the extra Maths classes but she should.
4. They _____ cakes all day.
5. He _____ his elderly neighbours to do their shopping.
6. _____ you _____ money to the Animal Rescue Centre?

Total: 5

Present perfect simple vs. present perfect continuous

6 Complete the sentences with the correct form of the verbs in brackets.
1. We _have raised_ (raise) £500 for charity.
2. He _____ (go) to the football club for nearly a year now.
3. You look really tired! How many exams _____ (have) this week?
4. I _____ (not sell) any tickets for the charity concert. Nobody's interested!
5. We _____ (pick) up rubbish from the beach every weekend since May.
6. How long _____ (they/help) at the youth club on Friday evenings?

Total: 5

24   Unit 2

Language builder

7 Circle the correct options.

Cath: ¹___ did you live before, Ned?
Ned: We ²___ live in the city centre. I loved it!
Cath: Why ³___ here, then?
Ned: Well, my granny ⁴___ ill in hospital, and after she got better she found it difficult to look after ⁵___ . We ⁶___ her in the summer holidays each year, but of course, that wasn't enough, so my parents decided to move near her.
Cath: ⁷___ this cottage? It's beautiful.
Ned: My parents ⁸___ home from my granny's house one weekend when they ⁹___ it. We only moved in a few days ago, that's why all our things are still in boxes! Those boxes are all my parents' books.
Cath: Wow, what a lot! How many books ¹⁰___ with them?
Ned: I've got no idea, hundreds, I suppose, but we ¹¹___ boxes ever since we arrived. We've got so much stuff that I ¹²___ found all my things!

		a		b		c
1	(a)	Where	b	When	c	What
2	a	would	b	had	c	used to
3	a	you came	b	did you come	c	had you come
4	a	had been	b	has been	c	had
5	a	himself	b	each other	c	herself
6	a	didn't use to visit	b	have visited	c	would visit
7	a	Who did you find	b	Who found	c	Who did find
8	a	drove	b	were driving	c	had driven
9	a	had seen	b	were seeing	c	saw
10	a	had they brought	b	have they brought	c	have they been bringing
11	a	've unpacked	b	've been unpacking	c	were unpacking
12	a	yet haven't	b	haven't already	c	still haven't

Total: 11

Vocabulary builder

8 Circle the correct options.

1 We were ___ by the small amount of money we raised. We'd expected more.
   (a) disappointed   b proud   c fascinated
2 I can't go camping. I haven't got a ___ .
   a sleeping bag   b water bottle   c pen-knife
3 She loves running. I've never known anyone so ___ about their sport.
   a shy   b passionate   c easy-going
4 The karaoke was fun, but using a ___ isn't as easy as it looks.
   a gallery   b microphone   c juggler
5 I need to quickly make ___ . Is that OK?
   a a mess   b my homework   c a phone call
6 I went on the Internet to ___ when the concert was.
   a pick up   b find out   c look up to
7 More people are ___ of the dark than you think.
   a keen   b afraid   c happy
8 I'd like to go ___ next weekend but there isn't any snow at the moment.
   a sailing   b trekking   c skiing
9 He was a ___ footballer but too lazy to do much training.
   a motivated   b strict   c talented
10 Those are nice boots. Are they made of ___ ?
   a leather   b silk   c flat

Total: 9

Speaking

9 Put the sentences in the correct order to make a conversation.

_1_ **A:** What's up Pam? You don't look very happy.
___ **A:** I know what you mean. Look, you don't need to worry. Just don't use your phone much if she's there. She'll soon forget.
___ **A:** Oh, you poor thing! What was it about?
___ **A:** Look, I'm sure she'll calm down soon. She always does.
___ **A:** Right! I'm sure it will be fine. Now, how can I make you feel better? Shall we go to the sports centre?
___ **B:** Yes, I suppose you're right. That's what happened last time!
___ **B:** Well, she doesn't realise how important my phone is. I'd be lost without it!
___ **B:** She says I use my phone too much, and she doesn't want to pay for it.
___ **B:** I've had another argument with my mum.

Total: 8

Total: 58

Unit 2   25

Get it right! Unit 2

Reflexive pronouns

Remember that:
- we use reflexive pronouns when the object of the verb is the same as the subject. We do not use object pronouns.
  ✓ I enjoyed the concert.
  ✓ I enjoyed **myself** (at the concert).
  ✗ I enjoyed ~~me~~ (at the concert).
- when a reflexive pronoun refers to more than one person, we use *-selves*, not *-selfs*.
  ✓ Did the boys enjoy **themselves** at the concert?
  ✗ Did the boys enjoy ~~themselfs~~ at the concert?

1 Complete the conversation with the correct pronouns. Check your spelling!

Rob: Hi Mary, did you enjoy ¹__yourself__ last weekend?
Mary: Well, it was OK. I went for a picnic with my friends on Saturday.
Rob: That sounds good!
Mary: Yes, but my friend Helen just talked about ²_____ all the time. I was bored.
Rob: What did you do on Sunday?
Mary: We went to play tennis, one of my brothers hurt ³_____ and we had to go home. My parents were out, so we had to look after ⁴_____ . I cooked dinner, and my brothers taught ⁵_____ to play a new video game.
Rob: Do you want to go to the cinema next weekend? That would be fun!
Mary: OK. Thanks! I'll see you next weekend. Bye!
Rob: Take care of ⁶_____ . Bye!

advice

Remember that:
- *advice* is an uncountable noun. It does not have a plural form with *-s* and we do not use *a/an* before it.
  ✓ I'm writing to thank you for your **advice** about my new school.
  ✗ I'm writing to thank you for your ~~advices~~ about my new school.
  ✓ My mum always gives me good **advice**.
  ✗ My mum always gives me ~~a~~ good advice.
- *advice* is the noun, but the verb is *advise*.
  ✓ He **advised** me to take the train to London.
  ✗ He ~~adviced~~ me to take the train to London.
  ✓ Thank you for your **advice**.
  ✗ Thank you for your ~~advise~~.

2 Find and correct five more mistakes with *advice* in the email.

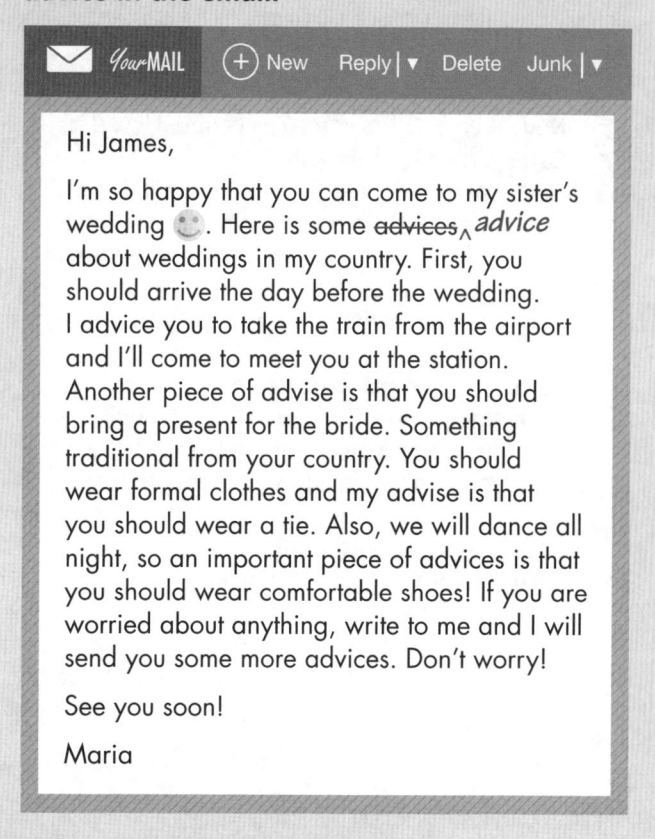

Hi James,

I'm so happy that you can come to my sister's wedding ☺. Here is some ~~advices~~ ^*advice* about weddings in my country. First, you should arrive the day before the wedding. I advice you to take the train from the airport and I'll come to meet you at the station. Another piece of advise is that you should bring a present for the bride. Something traditional from your country. You should wear formal clothes and my advise is that you should wear a tie. Also, we will dance all night, so an important piece of advices is that you should wear comfortable shoes! If you are worried about anything, write to me and I will send you some more advices. Don't worry!

See you soon!

Maria

Spell it right! Personal qualities

B1 and B2 students often make spelling mistakes when writing these adjectives for personal qualities from Unit 2. Remember to write them correctly.

hard-working   easy-going   sociable
strict   talented   (im)patient

3 Correct the spelling mistake in each sentence.

1 She's a very ~~hard worker~~ ^*hard-working* person and she practises every day.
2 They're a very tallented family – they all play a musical instrument.
3 Jane's a successful businesswoman and very hard working.
4 Her parents are very social. They've been out every night this week!
5 My teacher is sometimes impacient with us when we don't know the answers.
6 He's a very easy going person and always great fun.
7 My parents are quite strickt about what time I go to bed.

3 Young achievers

Vocabulary

Training and qualifications

1 ★ Put the sections in the correct order to make a text.
   a Most young people don't know what they want to do in life. Often finding a **career**
   b **fees**, but they didn't have much money, so I decided to try and look for a **part-time**
   c **exam**, but I passed and I've been a museum curator ever since!
   d **path** is more luck than anything, I think. When I left school, I started a **university**
   e **form**. The course only had twenty places, and to be accepted I had to take an **entrance**
   f **experience** for a historian and I loved it. Then the director suggested doing a **training**
   g **degree** in History, my favourite subject at school. My parents agreed to pay the **course**
   h **course** to be a museum curator. It sounded interesting, so I filled in the **application**
   i **job**. I was lucky. I got a job at the local museum giving guided tours. It was great **work**

   1 _a_ 2 ___ 3 ___ 4 ___ 5 ___
   6 ___ 7 ___ 8 ___ 9 ___

2 ★★ Complete the sentences. Use one or two words from Exercise 1 for each space.
   1 I can't decide if I want to go to _university_ and study for a degree, or try and find a job.
   2 When do I have to pay the _____ for next year?
   3 It says on your _____ that you have always been interested in computers.
   4 That university has a(n) _____ exam and it's really difficult to get a place there.
   5 I see you've done language _____ in French, Dutch and Spanish. How fluent are you?
   6 She's had so many different jobs it's difficult to see a clear career _____ .

3 ★★ Complete the job advert.

   Secondary school teachers needed

   We need both ¹ _full-time_ (40 hours a week) and ² _____ teachers (15 or 21 hours a week) for the next academic year. The ³ _____ is challenging and interesting, and every day is different. Teaching is a(n) ⁴ _____ where you can really make a difference!

   Qualifications:
   You need a teacher ⁵ _____ certificate in the subject you want to teach. Some ⁶ _____ working with children in a school environment is also an advantage, as is a university ⁷ _____ .

   Applications:
   Please download and complete the ⁸ _____ by visiting our webpage.

4 ★★★ Look at the jobs in the box. What do people need to do them in your country? How many words from Exercise 1 can you use?

   car mechanic   dentist   secondary school teacher
   radio presenter   hotel receptionist   pilot

   To be a dentist, you need a university degree and a year of practical experience.

Language focus 1

be going to and present tenses for the future

1 ★ Circle the correct options.
1. What time **are you meeting** / do you meet your friends at the library?
2. The exam tomorrow **is going to start / starts** at 8.30 am.
3. My sister **is going to do / is doing** work experience before her degree if she can.
4. The Young People of the Year Awards **take / are going to take** place this Friday.
5. Nathan **is going / is going to go** for a job interview this afternoon. He's very nervous!
6. No, we **aren't going / don't go** to see each other until Sunday.
7. I've decided **I'm studying / I'm going to study** computer science at university.
8. What day **does school finish / is school going to finish** this term?

2 ★★ Complete the text with the correct future form of the verbs in brackets.

LUCA, BASKETBALL PLAYER, ARGENTINA, 14

Q: What are you doing at the weekend?
A: I ¹ _'m playing_ (play) a league match on Saturday morning, and I ² _____ (go) to a party with some friends in the evening. On Sunday, I ³ _____ (not do) a lot. I ⁴ _____ (relax).

Q: And what are your plans for the summer?
A: In July, my team ⁵ _____ (take) part in an international tournament in Spain. It ⁶ _____ (start) at the end of June and ⁷ _____ (end) in early August.

Q: So, what about your future, Luca?
A: That's easy! I ⁸ _____ (work) hard and one day I ⁹ _____ (play) in the NBA.

---

3 ★★★ Complete the text with the correct future form of the verbs in the box.

| study   practise   prepare   go   ~~compete~~ |
| not get   participate   take |

Kaye Yao, 15, ¹ _is competing_ in the South Korean Sudoku Super Challenge this year with thousands of other teenage competitors. The event ² _____ place next December. Yao ³ _____ for the fourth time (last year she was third in her category). So, how ⁴ _____ she _____ for the championships? Well, she ⁵ _____ to a two-day training camp next November. Then she ⁶ _____ every day until the championships, but she ⁷ _____ nervous. 'I just do Sudoku for fun,' says Yao. 'I love logic and puzzles and I ⁸ _____ Maths at university.'

4 ★★★ Write answers to the questions.
1. When is the next birthday in your family and whose is it?
   _____
2. What are the dates of the next school holidays?
   _____
3. What arrangements have you got in the next few weeks, and who with?
   _____
4. What are your plans for the future?
   _____

My mum's birthday is on December 14th.

Explore expressions with take

5 ★★ Complete the text with the words in the box.

| time   the exams   ~~place~~   advice   up |

There's a big education fair in my city which takes ¹ _place_ in May each year. I'm going to go because I don't know what to do when I leave school. It's difficult to know who to take ² _____ from, because everyone tells me different things! Dad says I should take ³ _____ a job in the family business, like he did. My teachers think I should go to university, and Mum wants me to take ⁴ _____ to go to Oxford or Cambridge. I suppose I can take ⁵ _____ to decide what I want to do as I'm only 14, but I like to plan ahead!

Listening and vocabulary

Listening

1 ★ 🔊 03 **Listen to a journalist interviewing a child actress. Tick (✓) the plans Sarah has for the future.**

film acting ☐   stage acting ☐
writing ☐   a university course ☐

2 ★★ 🔊 03 **Listen again. Are these sentences true (T) or false (F)?**

1 Sarah made her first film when she was five. _F_
2 She didn't enjoy being in films when she started. ___
3 She wanted to go to high school and make friends. ___
4 When she was in films, she had tutors and no friends her own age. ___
5 She continued to have acting offers after she gave it up. ___
6 After she stopped acting, she still wanted to be rich and famous. ___
7 Her novel is about her problems with growing up. ___
8 She often can't decide what she wants to do. ___
9 She plans to write another novel. ___
10 She acted in lots of student productions at school. ___

Achievements

3 ★ **Match the verbs (1–8) with the words and phrases in the box.**

> records project fortune voluntary work
> ~~business~~ community millionaire awards

1 start a _business_
2 break _____
3 win _____
4 support the _____
5 become a _____
6 develop a _____
7 do _____
8 make a _____

4 ★★ **Complete the texts with the correct form of the expressions in Exercise 3.**

Usain Bolt worked hard to be a sprinter (his coach said he was too tall!), and won his first gold medal at 15. Since then he has ¹ _broken_ the world _record_ several times, and in the process he has ² _____ a multi-_____ . He now earns a salary of $20m a year, and though he doesn't have time to ³ _____ any _____ himself, he has given millions of dollars to charity.

Nowadays, many young people are trying to ⁴ _____ an online _____ , like Mark Zuckerberg did with Facebook. He ⁵ _____ the _____ for a social-networking site with some friends at university, and it was so successful that by the age of 23 he had ⁶ _____ . He's now a billionaire and Facebook has over a billion users.

Shakira, who had her first big hit in South America when she was only 19, has set up her own charity, Pies Descalzos, in Colombia. The charity ⁷ _____ poor children in _____ , and helps them to get an education. In 2014, she ⁸ _____ a Hero _____ at the Radio Disney Music Awards for her charity work.

Language focus 2

Predictions with *be going to*, *will* and *may/might*

1 ★★ Complete the predictions with the correct form of the verbs in brackets.
1. You've done a fantastic project! You *'ll win* (win) an award, I'm sure.
2. Next year, we _____ (have) enough money to open another shop. I hope so!
3. Now she's in the last 100 metres – she _____ (break) the world record by several seconds! Amazing!
4. They are so creative. I'm sure they _____ (be) a success.
5. She's on the last chapter of her novel now. I think she _____ (finish) it this week.
6. They _____ (win) the league, but they're not the only good team. It _____ (not be) easy.
7. The way things are going with the business, we _____ (not make) a fortune.
8. He's a great actor. He _____ (get) an Oscar one day, I know.

Future continuous

2 ★ Complete the rules in the table.

1	To form the future continuous, use *will* + _____ + _____ .
2	We use the future continuous to make _____ about the future.
3	We only use the future continuous with actions, not with _____ verbs.

3 ★★ Complete the sentences with the future continuous form of the verbs in the box.

| make   stay   do   not live   ~~study~~   work |

1. Next year, I *'ll be studying* at university in Paris, I hope.
2. My brother thinks he _____ a fortune soon. He's very ambitious.
3. In the future, more people _____ from home and sending emails to their bosses.
4. In a few years time, we _____ at home anymore.
5. _____ you _____ at school until you're 18?
6. If my application is successful, I _____ voluntary work in Africa next summer.

4 ★★ Join the parts of the sentences for each person.
Adrian:
1. We don't think he's going — *b*
2. He has lots of great ideas. He may ___
3. Soon he'll be ___

a. making a fortune, I'm sure.
b. to go to university. He wants to earn money.
c. try to develop one into an online business.

Gemma:
4. I think she's ___
5. As a female student, she'll ___
6. She's not sure, but that ___

d. enter a world of male students, I suppose.
e. might feel strange after an all-girl's school.
f. going to study engineering at university.

5 ★★ Circle the correct options in the text.

Kelvin Doe, from Sierra Leone, is a teenage engineer you [1]***'re going to hear*** / **might hear** a lot more about, for sure. A few years ago, he was the youngest person nominated for the 'Creative People in Business' award, and many people think he [2]**'ll win / 'll be winning** lots of major awards in the future. Kelvin's current project is to build a windmill. He hopes it [3]**'ll provide / 'll be providing** power for all his Freetown neighbours. Last summer, he worked on engineering projects at MIT in Boston, and his teachers hope that he [4]**might take / 's going to take** his degree there. Kelvin isn't sure, but he wants to become a scientist to improve life for the people of Sierra Leone, so he [5]**may decide / 's going to decide** that studying abroad is the best way. One thing is certain, though: Kelvin [6]**won't stay / might not stay** away for a long time because he loves Sierra Leone too much.

6 ★★★ Choose three of your friends. Make two predictions about each of them using the forms on this page.

Chloe might go and live abroad one day.

Reading

1 ★ Read the profiles of three teenagers and match them to their achievements.
Angela ___   Santiago ___   Charley ___
- a sport
- b physics
- c computer coding
- d medical research
- e gaming
- f teaching

TEENAGE ACHIEVERS

Angela Zhang recently finished high school in California, but she has already won a $100,000 award to study at university for her research on a nanoparticle system for treating cancer. Angela said she started developing the project in her first year at high school, reading bio-engineering articles and attending scientific **talks**. Later on, she did research in a laboratory at Stanford, where she successfully tested the system on mice. It might be years before we know if the system will work on humans, but she may be on the way to finding a **cure** for cancer. When she's not doing that, Angela is like any typical teenager. She loves buying shoes, and in her free time goes canoeing and walking.

Santiago Gonzalez is a 14-year-old computer scientist from Colorado, USA. He already attends university, and will graduate at 16, and complete his master's degree at 17. He's fluent in a dozen programming languages, and says that when he has a difficult programming problem, he will often dream the solution. Santiago happily calls himself a geek, and says that for him learning is as **essential** as eating. When he's not studying, he writes mobile apps. He's already developed about 15, including puzzles and games. His **ambition** is to work at Apple.

Charley Hull started playing golf when she was only 2, and was soon beating golfers much older than her. She had her first big success aged 9, when she won the English Amateur Ladies Championship. She started home schooling at 13 so she could travel to tournaments. In 2013, aged 17, Charley **turned** professional, and was voted the best new player, or 'rookie', of the European Tour. On the golf course, she's incredibly determined. Friends say, 'She's going to be world number 1!', and experts agree it may not take her very long. Off the golf course, she loves music, parties and being with her friends.

2 ★★ Complete the sentences with the correct form of the words in **bold** from the text.
1 If you want to be a doctor, it's _____ to go to university.
2 Being a pilot has been my _____ since I went on a plane for the first time.
3 At school we've had several careers _____ from people with different jobs.
4 My granny is planning a big celebration for next year when she _____ sixty.
5 Scientists make many discoveries, but they can't find a(n) _____ for the common cold!

3 ★★ Read the profiles again and answer the questions.
1 Who is studying at university?
   Angela and Santiago
2 Who has been given financial help to study? _____
3 Who likes doing typical teenage things? _____
4 Who finds the answers to difficult problems while sleeping? _____
5 Who won an adult competition at a very young age? _____
6 Who has a very clear career aim? _____
7 Who worked on a complicated project for several years? _____
8 Who left school early? _____
9 Who has developed things for people to have fun? _____
10 Who doesn't mind spending time always doing the same thing? _____

4 ★★★ Who are these people talking about? Write *Angela*, *Santiago* or *Charley*.
1 '_____ is going to make a fortune and become the best in the world.'
2 '_____ will be able to change many people's futures with this work.'
3 '_____ , with so many ideas, may be the head of our company one day.'
4 '_____ has had to be very motivated, but will see the benefits of this very soon.'
5 '_____ will be selling a lot of original products and will probably make a lot of money.'
6 '_____ has a long career ahead working on new techniques.'

5 ★★★ You have to choose the winner of the 'Young Person of the Year Award'. Who do you think should win – Angela, Santiago or Charley – and why? Write at least five sentences.

Writing

An opinion essay

1 Read the essay. Does the author agree or disagree with the opinion in the essay title?

School leavers should attend university before they start working. Do you agree?

The best students go to university. That's what everyone has always told us. ¹**Firstly, / (However,)** I don't think all school leavers should go to university before they start working.

²**In conclusion, / Firstly,** we have to ask ourselves why we would want to send all school leavers to do a university course. ³**Although / However,** these courses can be very useful and students can learn a lot, not all students are capable of studying at the level required by universities to become scientists, teachers or lawyers. ⁴**In addition, / Whereas** we also need people who are going to work in factories, repair machines or grow things for us to eat – important technical skills that don't require a degree.

Finally, ⁵**in addition, / whereas** there are a lot of school leavers who want to continue studying at a higher level, there are many who would rather start working immediately or do training for a practical skill. Not everyone wants to go to university.

⁶**In conclusion, / In addition,** I don't agree that all school leavers should go to university. A degree is the logical path for many students, but it's definitely not the *only* path.

2 Read the essay again. Tick (✓) the points the author makes.
1 Students can get a lot of knowledge from university courses. ✓
2 Not every school leaver wants to continue studying. ☐
3 Many school leavers don't have the correct academic level for university. ☐
4 Universities are often very expensive and not everyone can afford them. ☐
5 As well as professional people with university degrees, we also need people with other skills. ☐
6 Only university students will get the best jobs. ☐

Useful language Linking phrases

3 Read the essay again. Circle the correct options.

4 Complete this short essay with the linking phrases in the box.

> although   in conclusion   ~~firstly~~   in addition
> whereas   however

Students should learn financial skills at school

There are several points to consider. ¹ _Firstly_ , it is an important life skill to learn how to make financial decisions. ² _____ , we need to know what consequences our decisions about money will have. ³ _____ we handle money every day, many of us don't understand the value of money. Some people would argue we don't need to understand, ⁴ _____ others would say it's important to learn this early in life. ⁵ _____ , we cannot deny that basic financial skills can be important.

⁶ _____ , I believe that financial skills should be learned from a young age.

32   Unit 3

Writing

5 Circle the correct options.
1. No / **Not** everyone wants to learn skills like these.
2. Many / Much students want to continue learning.
3. Lot / Lots of people want to find a job quickly.
4. Only few / a few school leavers will end up in top jobs.
5. All / Every schools want the best for their students.
6. Some / Any people believe that students should stay in school longer.

6 Complete the sentences with the correct form of the verbs in the box.

| leave   think   ~~learn~~   study   do |

1. Many students would rather do a training course or ___learn___ a new skill.
2. Students have to make important decisions and _____ carefully.
3. Many people are going back to school or _____ courses.
4. Nowadays, most people study, whereas in the past many people got a job or _____ the country.
5. He didn't enjoy going to school or _____ .

> **WRITING TIP**
> Make it better! ✓ ✓ ✓
> Use different expressions to give your opinion.
> *I feel that work experience can often be more useful than formal training.*

7 Circle the correct words.
1. To / **In** my opinion, children leave school too early.
2. I **believe** / opinion it's important to learn social skills.
3. As far / much as I'm concerned, it's more important to get a good job.
4. Personally / Personal, I think that most students work very hard.
5. In my mean / view, students need practical skills as well as academic skills.

8 Match the paragraphs of an opinion essay (1–4) with the functions (a–d).
1. Introduction ___
2. Argument 1 ___
3. Argument 2 ___
4. Conclusion ___

a. Give another reason to support your opinion with examples.
b. Introduce the topic and give your opinion.
c. Give a summary of your reasons and give your opinion again in different words.
d. Give one reason to support your opinion with examples.

PLAN

9 You are going to write an opinion essay with the title: 'Exams are not the best way to test a student's ability.' Use the paragraphs in Exercise 8 and make notes.

WRITE

10 Write your opinion essay. Look at page 39 of the Student's Book to help you.

_____
_____
_____
_____
_____
_____
_____
_____
_____
_____
_____
_____
_____
_____

CHECK

11 Check your writing. Can you say YES to these questions?
- Have you used the essay structure in Exercise 8?
- Have you used linking phrases to make your essay clearer?
- Have you used the correct quantifiers to make general statements?
- Have you used the correct verb forms in lists with *and* or *or*?
- Have you used different expressions to give your personal opinion?
- Are the spelling and punctuation correct?

Do you need to write a second draft?

3 Review

Vocabulary
Training and qualifications

1 Circle the correct options.
1. I met my best friend at university. We were studying the same **degree** / **career path**.
2. To get my qualification, I had to do some **part-time job** / **work experience** in a big hotel.
3. She couldn't do the course because she couldn't afford the **university degree** / **course fees**.
4. Before you can go to that school you have to pass an **entrance exam** / **application form**.
5. Your **career path** / **training course** has been very unusual – you've had many different jobs.
6. When he was at college, he got a **course fees** / **part-time job** in a bookshop.

Total: 5

Achievements

2 Complete the texts with the phrases in the box. There are two extra phrases.

> a fortune   a project   ~~a business~~   the community
> awards   a millionaire   record   voluntary work

Lots of people start ¹ _a business_ but not many of them manage to make ² _____ . The English computer programmer Nick d'Aloisio did both. He created Summly, an app to summarise text, when he was 15, and started his own Internet company. In 2013, at the age of 18, he sold the company to Yahoo for $30m and became ³ _____ .

Malala Yousafzai is a Pakistani teenager who believes girls should have the same opportunities for education as boys. In her town she fought for girls to have support in ⁴ _____ so that they could continue their education. Malala has spoken at the United Nations and has been involved in developing ⁵ _____ to increase girls' education all over the world. She has won several ⁶ _____ , including the Nobel Peace Prize.

Total: 5

Language focus
be going to and present tenses for the future

3 Complete the conversations with the correct future form of the verb in brackets.
1. 'Have you got any plans for the summer?'
   'Yes, I _'m going to spend_ (spend) July with my cousins.'
2. 'Is the awards ceremony on TV tonight?'
   'Yes, it _____ (start) at 7pm.'
3. 'What time _____ (his train/get) here?'
   'It _____ (arrive) at 7 o'clock.'
4. 'Is it true? _____ (you/go) for a job interview today?'
   'Yes, I _____ (try) to earn some money before university.'

Total: 5

Predictions with be going to, will and may/might

4 Circle the correct options.
1. She **might** / **will** win the Nobel Prize but there are lots of other good people.
2. You **'re not going to** / **might not** break the record today. It's much too windy.
3. I think he **may** / **will** get a good degree and find a good job. He's a brilliant student.
4. She **might** / **'s going to** find a part-time job this summer but it isn't easy.
5. They're top and there's only one match left. They **'re going to** / **may** win the league!
6. I think I **'ll** / **'m going to** have a big family.

Total: 5

Future continuous

5 Write future continuous sentences with the prompts.
1. We / break / records / with this project
   We'll be breaking records with this project.
2. They / not make / a fortune / with that crazy idea!
   _____
3. He / star / in Hollywood films / in a year or two
   _____
4. She / start / her own company / in a couple of years
   _____
5. people / buy / this product / in five years' time?
   _____

Total: 4

Language builder

6 Circle the correct options.

Ainan Cawley was an unusual baby. When he ¹___ eight months old, he ²___ to walk and run, and by one year he ³___ like an adult. By the age of six, he was a chemistry prodigy and from the age of eight he ⁴___ to a university chemistry laboratory several times a week. He also taught ⁵___ biology and how to write computer code. Ainan is now a teenager. He ⁶___ live in Singapore, but now he lives in Malaysia and he ⁷___ to university there since he was eleven. Ainan isn't just a scientist, however. He ⁸___ several film scores, learned to play the piano, and in 2013 he directed his first short film. What will he do next? He ⁹___ become a scientist doing research, or he could choose a career in the arts. One thing is sure, though: Ainan ¹⁰___ to surprise us for many years to come!

#	a	b	c
1	had been	(b) was	has been
2	had learned	has learned	is learning
3	has talked	was talking	had talked
4	go	used to be	would go
5	himself	each other	yourself
6	had	would	used to
7	has been going	is going	went
8	is composing	has composed	has been composing
9	might	will	going to
10	continues	may continue	will be continuing

Total: 9

Vocabulary builder

7 Circle the correct options.

1 This charity is trying to ___ young people with no work in the community.
   a develop   (b) support   c make
2 I'm really excited ___ getting this award.
   a about   b for   c with
3 When is the entrance ___ for the college?
   a form   b exam   c fees
4 People said I was too young to ___ a company, but they were wrong.
   a bring together   b sign up   c set up
5 I think she'll probably ___ a millionaire with this invention.
   a make   b become   c win
6 It was difficult but I was determined to do ___ .
   a a mistake   b a fortune   c the right thing
7 I didn't ___ him because he got so impatient.
   a happy with   b get on with   c come back
8 It's ___ to find out how many young achievers there are!
   a terrified   b excited   c interesting

Total: 7

Speaking

8 Circle the correct phrases to complete the conversation.

Mark: ¹(We need to decide)/ I'd rather how to choose this year's Student of the Year.

Will: Yes, I ²was thinking of / think the best way is to ask everyone to suggest other students.

Mark: OK, but that might take a long time.

Will: ³How shall we decide / What kind of thing, then?

Mark: Well, ⁴that's a good idea / I was thinking of suggesting a category for this year's award. What do you think?

Will: OK, ⁵what kind of thing / how shall we decide do you suggest?

Mark: Maybe it could be students who've collected money for charity.

Will: I don't know. Personally, ⁶I'd rather / we need to decide focus on people who do a lot of voluntary work.

Mark: Yes, ⁷that's a good idea / I think the best way is, too.

Total: 6

Total: 46

Get it right! Unit 3

be going to for the future

Remember that:
- we use **subject + the present tense of be + going to + infinitive** to talk about future plans and intentions. Remember to use the correct form of *be* and the infinitive.
  - ✓ *I'm going to start driving lessons as soon as I can!*
  - ✗ *I going to start driving lessons as soon as I can!*
  - ✗ *I'm going to starting driving lessons as soon as I can!*
  - ✗ *I'm going to started driving lessons as soon as I can!*
- we use **the present tense of be + subject** after question words, e.g. *why, what, when, where, how*.
  - ✓ *What are you going to buy?*
  - ✗ *What you are going to buy?*

1 Circle the correct option.
1. What film **we are** / **are we** / **we** going to see this afternoon?
2. I'm going to **get** / **getting** / **got** a good job after school.
3. They **are going** / **going** / **is going** to go to university next year.
4. What **you are** / **are you** / **you** going to do when you finish school?
5. My best friend, Amy, is going to **study** / **studied** / **studying** History at university.
6. We are going to **spent** / **spending** / **spend** the summer holidays in Miami.
7. Where **is he** / **he is** / **he** going to meet his sister?
8. He is going to **travelled** / **travel** / **travelling** before he goes to university.

Predictions with *will*

Remember that:
- we use **will + infinitive** to make a general prediction or to give an opinion about the future.
  - ✓ *I think you will like my new car when you see it.*
  - ✗ *I think you like my new car when you see it.*
- we make predictions with **will/won't** when we feel sure about a future action or event.

2 Write sentences about the future with *will*. Use the words given and *will*.
1. I / think / my country / be / different / in 20 years
   I think my country will be different in 20 years.
2. My brother / be / successful / in the future
   _____
3. I'm sure / you / enjoy / your new job
   _____
4. If it / rains, / we / have lunch / at my house
   _____
5. They / meet / us / at the station / at 4 o'clock
   _____
6. I / promise / you / that you / not forget / your visit
   _____

Confusing words: *job, work, career, course*

Remember that:
- we use *job* to talk about the regular work that a person does to earn money.
  - ✓ *It's a good idea to get a part-time job.*
  - ✗ *It's a good idea to get a part-time work.*
- we use *work* to talk about the activity that someone does in their job.
  - ✓ *His boss thanked him for all his hard work.*
  - ✗ *His boss thanked him for all his hard job.*
- we use *career* to talk about a job or series of similar jobs that you do during your working life.
  - ✓ *It's an interesting career and well-paid.*
  - ✗ *It's an interesting course and well-paid.*
- we use *course* to talk about a set of lessons or a plan of study on a particular subject, usually leading to an exam or qualification.
  - ✓ *I want to get a job after I finish my course.*
  - ✗ *I want to get a job after I finish my career.*

3 Complete the sentences with the correct word – *job, work, course,* or *career*.
1. My mum goes to ___work___ from Monday to Thursday.
2. You should go swimming or play tennis after _____ .
3. If you study hard, you will be able to get a good _____ when you leave school.
4. I'm going to start a _____ in Business English because I want to work in England.
5. She wants to find a new _____ as a doctor in the USA.
6. She worked hard in her _____ and had a great _____ .

4 Fabulous food

Vocabulary
Cooking verbs

1 ★ Put the letters in order to make ten cooking verbs.

1 pcoh _chop_
2 sadrep _____
3 ryf _____
4 bilo _____
5 selic _____
6 taros _____
7 ligrl _____
8 imx _____
9 keab _____
10 tager _____

2 ★ Look at the photos and complete the sentences.

1 My grandfather _slices_ his _bread_ really thin, it's amazing.
2 It doesn't take long to _____ a strawberry _____ .
3 How can you _____ _____ without crying?
4 My mum always _____ _____ for Sunday lunch.
5 I can't cook much but I can _____ things like _____ .
6 I usually _____ butter and _____ on my toast.
7 It's easy to _____ _____ and tomato to make a toasted sandwich.
8 My mum _____ _____ for exactly 3½ minutes.
9 We sometimes _____ _____ with honey and nuts to have for dessert.
10 When I make cakes, I _____ _____ into the mixture.

3 ★★ Complete the recipes with words from Exercise 1. You can use the words more than once.

Easy pizza recipe
First, ¹_spread_ the tomato sauce thickly over the pizza base. ²_____ the onions, red pepper and mushrooms thinly. Then, ³_____ the onion and tomato rings over the tomato sauce. Finally, ⁴_____ the cheese, and put it over the vegetables. ⁵_____ the pizza in the oven for 10–15 minutes.

Potato salad
⁶_____ the potatoes, carrots and peas until cooked, and the eggs in a separate pan. When cool, ⁷_____ the potatoes, carrots and eggs into small pieces. Finally, ⁸_____ all the ingredients together with mayonnaise, salt and pepper.

Macaroni cheese bake
First, ⁹_____ the macaroni in salty water, then put it in a frying pan with lots of tomato sauce. Then, ¹⁰_____ the macaroni for a few minutes in the pan. Then, put it in a dish, grate or slice some cheese and ¹¹_____ it over the top. Finally, ¹²_____ it in the oven or ¹³_____ it until the cheese turns golden brown.

4 ★★★ Write about your favourite dish and how to cook it.

My favourite dish is _____ .
To make it, you'll need _____
_____ .
First, _____
_____ .
Then, _____
_____ .
Finally, _____
_____ .

My favourite dish is chicken risotto. To make it, you'll need rice, chopped cooked chicken, chopped onion, …

Unit 4 37

Language focus 1

First conditional with *if*, *when* and *unless*

1 ★★ Complete the first conditional sentences with *if*, *when* or *unless*.
1. Mum, will you get me some crisps ___when___ you go to the supermarket? Thanks!
2. _____ anyone is a vegetarian, I'll buy pepperoni pizzas.
3. I might buy some frozen peas _____ there aren't any green beans.
4. _____ you eat your vegetables, you won't have any dessert.
5. _____ Dad gets home, he'll put the macaroni cheese in the oven. He won't be long.
6. Will you grill the steak _____ I make the salad?

2 ★★ Write first conditional sentences with the prompts.
1. When / they / bring / the ingredients / I / make / the cake
   When they bring the ingredients, I'll make the cake.
2. The chips / burn / unless / you / fry / them gently
   _____
3. If / Paula / cook / tonight / she / make / spaghetti / again
   _____
4. you / help / me / with the recipe / when / I / cook supper / tonight?
   _____
5. Unless / they / remember / to buy / more bread / we / not have / enough
   _____
6. If / he / slice / the tomatoes / with that knife / he / cut / his finger
   _____

3 ★★ Circle the correct options to complete the mini-conversations.

Waiter: The menu's in Spanish, so I ¹explain / **'ll explain** if there's anything you ²don't understand / won't understand.
Jane: Thanks, but we're fine.

Ruth: Sorry, we haven't decided yet.
Waiter: That's OK. No hurry. I'll come back ³when / if you're ready to order.

Ruth: Mmm. Those mussels look delicious.
Jane: But aren't you allergic to shellfish? You ⁴'re / might be really sick if you ⁵eat / 'll eat them.

Ruth: ⁶When / Unless I finish this, I ⁷ask / 'll ask for the dessert menu, I think.
Jane: I don't know how you can eat so much!

Jane: ⁸If / Unless the waiter ⁹brings / will bring the bill soon, we'll be late for the cinema.
Ruth: Stop worrying. Here he comes.

4 ★★★ Complete the text with *if*, *when* and *unless* and the correct form of the verbs in brackets.

There's a lot of advice on the Internet about what food is good or bad for you. Things like:
'If you ¹___eat___ (eat) too many eggs, you ²_____ (have) high cholesterol.' 'You ³_____ (not get) heart problems ⁴_____ you eat a low-fat diet.' 'If you ⁵_____ (eat) a lot of garlic, it ⁶_____ (protect) you from illness.' 'You'll put on weight ⁷_____ you eat lots of fruit and vegetables.' 'If your food ⁸_____ (contain) a lot of sugar, you'll develop diabetes.'
But ⁹_____ you actually check these claims, you ¹⁰_____ (find) that they're not completely true. In fact ¹¹_____ you look carefully at the evidence, you'll realise that it's much more complicated than that. So stop worrying. If you eat a good, balanced diet, you ¹²_____ (not have) any problems.

5 ★★★ Complete the sentences for you.
1. When I start living on my own, I won't be able to _____ .
2. I'll make my own breakfast on Sunday unless _____ .
3. If I go to a restaurant for my next birthday, _____ .
4. _____ if I have to cook this weekend.
5. When I'm older and do all my own cooking, I might _____ .

When I start living on my own, I won't be able to make very many dishes.

Listening and vocabulary

Adjectives describing food

1 ★ **Complete the definitions with adjectives describing food.**

1 Something __salty__ has a lot of salt in it.
2 Something _____ tastes very good. 
3 Something _____ has salt not sugar in it. 
4 Something _____ isn't sweet. 
5 Something _____ has a lot of sugar in it. 
6 Something _____ doesn't taste good. 
7 Something _____ makes a noise when you eat it. 
8 Something _____ doesn't taste of anything. 
9 Something _____ is soft and oily and not nice. 
10 Something _____ tastes hot when you eat it. 

2 ★★ **Circle the correct words.**

1 You said you could cook! This chicken is (disgusting) / savoury. I can't eat it.
2 I hate sardines. It's the texture, not the taste, they're really **slimy** / **bitter**.
3 Little children usually like **salty** / **bland** food, without a strong taste.
4 I prefer **sweet** / **savoury** snacks, like nuts and crisps, rather than **sweet** / **savoury** ones, like chocolate bars.
5 My sister is a really good cook. Everything she makes is **slimy** / **delicious**.
6 It's hard to eat crisps secretly. They're so **spicy** / **crunchy** everyone can hear you!
7 I don't like dark chocolate. It has a **bitter** / **delicious** taste. I prefer milk chocolate.
8 This omelette is really **sweet** / **salty**. Why did you put so much salt in?

Listening

3 ★ 🔊 04 **Listen to a radio programme. What exactly did the man eat recently?**

4 ★★ 🔊 04 **Listen again and complete the sentences.**

1 Matt Sanchez makes hot __barbecue sauces__ .
2 Matt has been visiting the Fiery Foods Festival for _____ .
3 All the products there are flavoured with _____ .
4 Chilli peppers first grew in _____ , where children eat hot food and _____ .
5 Wilbur Scoville invented a way to work out _____ .
6 The hottest chillies are _____ Scoville units.
7 The competition involved eating _____ Carolina Reapers in the _____ possible.
8 Eating _____ or boiled _____ or drinking _____ first can help.
9 The winner took _____ to eat the Reapers.
10 The best thing to eat when your mouth is burning is _____ .

Unit 4   39

Language focus 2

Second conditional with *could* and *might*

1 ★ Circle the correct words in the table.

1	Use the second conditional to talk about situations that are **real / imaginary**.
2	To form the second conditional, use *if* + the **present simple / past simple** for the situation, and **would, could or might / will or won't** for a possible consequence.
3	To form questions, use (question word) + **would / will** + subject + verb.
4	*If* **can / can't** come at the beginning or in the middle of the sentence/question.

2 ★ Match the sentence beginnings (1–6) with the sentence endings (a–f).

1. I couldn't work in a restaurant _b_
2. If you gave up fizzy drinks, ___
3. If you could eat anything now, ___
4. My sister would eat crisps for breakfast ___
5. We could make a cake ___
6. I wouldn't eat broccoli ___

a. what would it be?
b. if I tried. It's a horrible job.
c. if we had some flour.
d. unless someone made me.
e. you might feel much healthier.
f. if my mum didn't stop her.

3 ★★ Complete the second conditional sentences. Use the modal verbs in brackets.

1. I can't buy everyone an ice cream because I haven't got enough money. (would)
   I ___would buy___ everyone an ice cream if I ___had___ enough money.
2. I'm not very hungry. That's why I maybe won't eat anything. (might)
   If I _____ hungry,
   I _____ something.
3. She doesn't know how to cook, so she isn't able to make lunch. (might)
   If she _____ how to cook,
   she _____ lunch.
4. He doesn't eat goat's cheese because he has a choice. (would)
   He _____ goat's cheese unless he _____ no choice.
5. There isn't a pizza delivery service here, so we can't order one. (could)
   If _____ a pizza delivery service,
   we _____ one.

4 ★★★ Complete the text with the words in the box. There are two you don't need to use.

> could ask   asked   might be   ~~was/were~~
> wouldn't be   would do   did   would have
> could discover   would like   wouldn't like
> prepared   stopped   would stop

If I ¹___was/were___ the head teacher of my school, I ²_____ something about school dinners. I ³_____ my mum to give the cooks some advice. I'm sure if I ⁴_____ her, she ⁵_____ lots of good ideas. I know, some students ⁶_____ happy if the cooks ⁷_____ serving chips with everything, like they do now, but it ⁸_____ healthier to do that. I also think people ⁹_____ it if the cooks ¹⁰_____ food from a different country or culture once a week. If they ¹¹_____ this, everyone ¹²_____ great new foods and recipes.

Explore prepositional phrases

5 ★ Complete the phrases with the prepositions in the box.

> on (x2)   in   by

1. ___on___ the streets
2. _____ many different ways
3. surrounded _____
4. _____ the go

6 ★★ Complete the sentences with the phrases in Exercise 5.

1. ___On the streets___ of Amsterdam you can buy chips with mayonnaise, spicy croquettes or herrings.
2. I never get bored with potatoes. You can cook them _____ .
3. When I'm _____ , my favourite street food is falafel.
4. My idea of paradise is to be _____ chocolate.

Reading

1 ★ **Read the article about food in space. Is it still very different from food on Earth?**

WHAT'S ON THE SPACE MENU TODAY?

Space food used to be boring. Astronauts ate food in bland powders and small cubes, and drank thick liquids from metal tubes. It was like science fiction. If you go into space nowadays, though, you'll eat lots of real food. The International Space Station, or ISS, has astronauts from the USA, Russia, Canada, Europe, China and Japan, who all like different things and eat three meals a day in a personalised menu which repeats every eight days. Each person selects their food in tasting sessions before they go into space, and nowadays there are a wide variety of *tasty* meals and snacks to choose from. The astronauts can choose from pasta or rice, fruit, vegetables, cereal, soup, meat, seafood, yoghurt, nuts, biscuits and more. Drinks include coffee, teas and fruit juice, but no fizzy drinks.

Space food comes in *disposable* packages, and how much preparation it needs on the space station depends on the kind of food. Some foods, like biscuits and fruit, can be eaten out of the packet. Others, such as scrambled eggs, macaroni cheese or rice, are mixed with water, and some, like meat, need to be heated up. There's an oven on the space station to bake things, but there's no fridge, so the food must be carefully prepared and vacuum-packed on Earth so that it will stay fresh.

One strange effect of the microgravity in space is that astronauts have a reduced sense of taste, so all food tastes blander than it would on Earth. For that reason, salty or spicy *seasoning* is really important. Astronauts use a lot of sauces, like chilli pepper sauce, soy sauce, ketchup, mayonnaise and mustard. Salt and pepper are available too, but only in liquid form. If astronauts *sprinkled* salt and pepper on their food in space like we do on Earth, it would just *float away*, and it could damage equipment or get stuck in an astronaut's eyes or nose. Although eating in space nowadays isn't quite like science fiction, it's still not easy!

2 ★ **Complete the definitions with the correct form of the words in bold from the text.**

1 We usually use _____ things once and then throw them away.
2 Food which is _____ is really good to eat.
3 When something moves easily up through the air, like a balloon, it _____ .
4 Salt, pepper, spices and herbs are different kinds of _____ .
5 When we _____ seasoning on food, we gently drop powder or liquid over it.

3 ★★ **Read the article again and answer the questions.**

1 Why did food in space use to be like science fiction?
   <u>Because it was all in powders, small cubes and metal tubes.</u>
2 Why does each astronaut have their own personalised menu?
   _____
3 Why do they have tasting sessions?
   _____
4 Why is seasoning important in space?
   _____
5 Why is salt and pepper on the space station liquid?
   _____

4 ★★ **Complete the information for new astronauts with the words in the box.**

| first day   eight   with water   fridge |
| three meals   heated up   stays fresh |
| of the packet   packaging   on Earth   drinks (x2) |

ISS FOOD FACT FILE
NASA

Menus: ¹ _Three meals_ a day + snacks for
² _____ days.
Then menu goes back to the
³ _____ .
Choose your menus ⁴ _____ .
You will also need to choose
⁵ _____ to go with the food.
All food comes in disposable
⁶ _____ so it ⁷ _____ .
Food may be eaten out ⁸ _____
or mixed ⁹ _____ or
¹⁰ _____ .
On the ISS there are no fizzy
¹¹ _____ , and there is no
¹² _____ .

5 ★★★ **What do you think the biggest problems with food would be for astronauts who had to live in space for several months? What three foods couldn't you live without if you were an astronaut? Write at least five sentences.**

Writing

Describing a local dish

1 Read the description of a local dish. What's the connection between the dish in the picture and the weather in Ireland?

I'm from Ireland and there are two things we love: potatoes and lamb. We eat lots of potatoes and there are lots of sheep in Ireland, so Irish stew is one of our favourite dishes. A stew ¹ _consists_ of meat and vegetables which are cooked together slowly in a tasty sauce. Irish stew ² _____ lamb, potatoes, carrots and onions. It has everything, but it is often ³ _____ with thick slices of brown bread spread with lots of butter.

Nobody knows who first made Irish stew but because the weather in Ireland is cold and wet, people usually eat a stew on a cold, rainy day. Traditional Irish cooking has many different kinds of stews – with beef, lamb, sausages or fish. People used to make stew over a fire but now it's easier to make on a cooker!

Irish stew is ⁴ _____ in pubs and restaurants all around Ireland, and it's not just for tourists! If you ever go to Ireland, it will probably rain, so try Irish stew for lunch to keep you warm.

2 Read the description again. Answer the questions.
1 Which two ingredients in Irish stew do Irish people particularly like?
They like potatoes and lamb.
2 What are the other ingredients of Irish stew?
_____
3 Who invented Irish stew?
_____
4 What other ingredients might you find in stews in Ireland?
_____
5 How did they make Irish stew in the past?
_____
6 Where can you eat it?
_____

Useful language Cooking and eating

3 Complete the description with the words in the box.

| served   consists   contains   made |

4 Match the sentence beginnings (1–6) with the sentence endings (a–f).
1 Paella is a Spanish dish which consists   _b_
2 Chicken nuggets contain   ___
3 A calzone is pizza bread filled   ___
4 Traditional fish and chips are made   ___
5 Meat and fish are usually served   ___
6 A pie is a pastry dish with fruit or meat baked   ___

a in a chip shop or 'chippy'.
b of rice with seafood and meat.
c in an oven.
d with ham, mushrooms and cheese.
e parts of a chicken you wouldn't normally eat.
f with potatoes in Ireland.

5 Complete the sentences with the correct form of the verb *be*.
1 These dishes __are__ served only in the most expensive restaurants in the world.
2 The stew can _____ cooked over a fire.
3 The meat _____ fried before we mix in the vegetables.
4 The cake _____ baked for 30 minutes and then we took it out.
5 Some snacks _____ served in the hotel garden before we sat down to lunch.

Writing

> **WRITING TIP**
>
> Make it better! ✓✓✓
> We only use *used to* for past habits. For present habits, we use the present simple with *usually*.
> I **used to** eat a lot of fish when I was younger.
> I **usually** go out for dinner with my family on special occasions.

6 Circle the correct options.
1 In the past, people **used to** / **usually** eat a lot less sugar.
2 Athletes **used to** / **usually** have a very strict diet nowadays.
3 Traditionally, bread **used to** / **usually** be baked once or twice a week.
4 My dad **used to** / **usually** have two cups of coffee in the morning but not anymore.
5 I **used to** / **usually** eat fish two or three times a week. I really like it!

> **WRITING TIP**
>
> Make it better! ✓✓✓
> End your description with a recommendation for the reader.
> *It's a wonderful idea to try local food when you travel to new places.*

7 Read the sentences. Which one is the strongest recommendation?
1 If you ever go to Dublin, you should try a full Irish breakfast.
2 I suggest you try it with a nice salad.
3 Why not go to a local restaurant and try a typical fish dish?
4 You could have this dish the next time you're in Istanbul.
5 This dish is absolutely delicious with rice – you really have to try it!

8 Look back at the description in Exercise 1. Complete the plan with the phrases in the box.

> a recommendation
> ~~the name of the dish~~
> how people cooked the dish in the past
> who invented it
> how to cook the dish
> where you can eat or buy it
> what the ingredients are
> why it's so popular

Paragraph 1 ¹*the name of the dish*
2 _____
3 _____
Paragraph 2 ⁴_____
5 _____
6 _____
Paragraph 3 ⁷_____
8 _____

PLAN

9 Think about a traditional dish from another country that you like. Use the plan in Exercise 8 and make notes.

WRITE

10 Write a description of the dish. Look at page 49 of the Student's Book to help you.

CHECK

11 Check your writing. Can you say YES to these questions?
- Have you used the ideas in Exercise 8?
- Have you used the phrases for cooking and eating in Exercise 3?
- Have you used the correct form of *be* in the phrases?
- Have you used *used to* and *usually* correctly?
- Have you finished the description with a recommendation?
- Are the spelling and punctuation correct?

Do you need to write a second draft?

4 Review

Vocabulary
Cooking verbs

1 Cross out the word in each sentence which is **not** correct.
1. How do you like your eggs? Shall I **fry / boil / grill** them?
2. First, **chop / mix / slice** the onions with a sharp knife.
3. I think we should **grate / bake / grill** the fish. It's healthier than frying.
4. **Fry / Boil / Roast** the meat with a little oil.
5. We need to **spread / chop / grate** the cheese all over the pizza.
6. The recipe says we must **boil / bake / roast** it in the oven until it's golden brown.
7. **Spread / Mix / Slice** the mixture with a spoon.
8. Can you **slice / grate / spread** the carrots to put in the salad?

Total: 7

Adjectives describing food

2 Complete the sentences with the words in the box.

| savoury disgusting bland spicy crunchy |
| salty delicious slimy bitter sweet |

1. Some seafood is very ___salty___ . I suppose it's because of the seawater!
2. They don't like honey. It's too _____ for them.
3. The food at that restaurant was _____ . I want my money back!
4. Little children prefer _____ food which hasn't got a strong taste.
5. Raw fish and oysters are very _____ , but they taste good!
6. I don't like sweet things like cakes and desserts, I prefer _____ food.
7. Mmmm, this cake is really _____ ! Can you give me the recipe?
8. It's difficult to eat _____ food like crisps quietly.
9. You didn't put any sugar in this. It tastes really _____ .
10. In India and Mexico the food is very _____ .

Total: 9

Language focus
First conditional with *if*, *when* and *unless*

3 Write first conditional sentences with *if*, *when* or *unless* and the prompts.
1. ___ / you / organise the drinks / we / get / the savoury snacks
   If you organise the drinks, we'll get the savoury snacks.
2. ___ / you / want / to do it yourself / I / make / the birthday cake
3. I / put / the food in the oven / ___ / your friends / arrive / for the party
4. What a big pizza! You / not be able to / eat it all / ___ / I / help / you!
5. Don't worry! I / ring / you / ___ / I / get / home from the restaurant
6. ___ / she / eat / any more crisps / she / might / not want / any supper

Total: 5

Second conditional with *could* and *might*

4 Circle the correct options in the text.
I ¹(would do)/ did a cooking course if I ²might have / had enough money. I've thought about it a lot. If I ³needed / wouldn't need to practise, I ⁴cooked / could cook for my friends and family. Then I ⁵'d feel / felt more confident as a cook – unless you ⁶wouldn't like / didn't like my cooking of course, but I can't imagine that! Then, if I ⁷could pass / passed the course, I ⁸'d look / looked for a job in a good restaurant. If that ⁹could go / went well, I ¹⁰might open / opened my own restaurant. If I ¹¹would own / owned a restaurant, I ¹²could get / got a Michelin star one day – why not? And if I ¹³would become / became a famous chef, I ¹⁴would appear / appeared on TV and travel around the world. But I ¹⁵couldn't do / didn't do any of this unless I ¹⁶might have / had the money for the cooking course. So, can you lend me the money?

Total: 15

Language builder

5 Circle the correct options.

Presenter:	Jimmy, is it true that you and Daniel taught ¹___ to cook?	
Jimmy:	Not really, we went to cookery college! We ²___ share a house with some other students and spend hours in the kitchen!	
Presenter:	And ³___ have you been managing restaurants together?	
Jimmy:	⁴___ about fifteen years.	
Presenter:	How many restaurants ⁵___ in that time?	
Jimmy:	Six, so far. We ⁶___ our seventh restaurant in the next few months if everything goes well.	
Presenter:	If you had the chance, ⁷___ start a restaurant abroad?	
Jimmy:	Actually, Daniel ⁸___ at some restaurants in New York next month. So I think we ⁹___ our first restaurant in the USA quite soon!	
Presenter:	¹⁰___ to stop expanding one day?	
Jimmy:	Well, if we want to maintain our quality, we ¹¹___ need to keep the business small. So ¹²___ we put a limit on new restaurants, it will be very difficult to visit them all regularly.	

	a	b	c
1	yourself	himself	yourselves
2	would	used to	was
3	where	how many	how long
4	Since	For	Already
5	have you been opening	have you opened	had you opened
6	will be opening	won't open	are opening
7	will you	would you	are you going to
8	is going to look	would look	looks
9	might open	won't open	would open
10	Will you	Are you going	Will you be going
11	would	could	will
12	unless	if	when

Total: 11

Vocabulary builder

6 Circle the correct options.
1 I was really disappointed ___ the new supermarket.
   a by   **b** for   **c** at
2 To become a chef, take a ___ in a cookery school.
   a training course   **b** part-time job   **c** work experience
3 Can you ___ this cheese to put on the pizzas?
   a mix   **b** grate   **c** spread
4 I love the ___ shirt he's wearing. It's so cool!
   a flat   **b** leather   **c** denim
5 If you want to be a top chef, you have to be ___ .
   a talented   **b** sociable   **c** easy-going
6 He has won a lot of ___ for his barbecue sauce.
   a fortune   **b** records   **c** awards
7 If you don't ___ the gas, you'll burn the onions.
   a save   **b** turn down   **c** reduce
8 This chocolate cake mix is too ___ . We need to add more sugar.
   a savoury   **b** bitter   **c** sweet

Total: 7

Speaking

7 Complete the conversation with the phrases in the box.

> need to stir   finally, when   next, you
> thing to do is   first of all, chop   then, add

Nina: So, Kate, how do I make the chocolate sauce for the ice cream?
Kate: OK, it's easy. The first ¹ _thing to do is_ get all the ingredients ready.
Nina: OK, I've got them here.
Kate: Great. So, ² _____ the chocolate into small pieces. ³ _____ put them in a bowl over a pan of boiling water. You ⁴ _____ it occasionally. OK?
Nina: Yes, I've written that down. Then what?
Kate: Put the cream in a saucepan and ⁵ _____ the sugar. Heat it up slowly, and stir it all the time so it doesn't burn. ⁶ _____ the mixture boils, pour it over the chocolate and mix everything together.

Total: 5

Total: 59

Get it right! Unit 4

Second conditional

> Remember that:
> - we use *if* + subject + past simple in the action/situation clause.
>   - ✓ *If you didn't need to study this evening, what would you do instead?*
> - we use *would/wouldn't* + infinitive to talk about the consequences. We don't use *will*.
>   - ✓ *If you didn't need to study this evening, what would you do instead?*
>   - ✗ *If you didn't need to study this evening, what will you do instead?*
> - we do not use *would/wouldn't* + infinitive in the same clause as *if*.
>   - ✓ *If you didn't need to study this evening, what would you do instead?*
>   - ✗ *If you wouldn't need to study this evening, what would you do instead?*
> - we form questions with *would(n't)* + subject + verb.
>   - ✓ *What would you do if you didn't need to study?*
>   - ✗ *What you would do if you didn't need to study?*

1 Are the sentences correct? Correct the incorrect sentences.

1. If you would add salt, it tasted better.
   If you added salt, it would taste better.
2. What you will cook if you could cook anything you wanted?
   _____
3. It would be nicer if you put grated cheese on it.
   _____
4. The coffee would be less bitter if you would added more sugar to it.
   _____
5. If you would eat a poisonous mushroom, you will be very ill.
   _____
6. Would you eat fugu fish if it will be on the menu?
   _____

Prepositions: *in* or *on*?

> Remember that:
> - we use *in* with places like countries, towns and buildings, and with containers.
>   - ✓ *Fugu fish is a delicacy in Japan.*
>   - ✗ *Fugu fish is a delicacy on Japan.*
> - we use *on* with flat or nearly flat surfaces.
>   - ✓ *What influences the food on your plate?*
>   - ✗ *What influences the food in your plate?*

2 Complete the sentences with *in* or *on*.

1. I would order it if it was ___*on*___ the menu.
2. They cook food _____ hot rocks _____ this country.
3. We bake our pizzas _____ a special oven.
4. Tourists in Cornwall eat pasties _____ the beach.
5. People _____ Japan live a long time because they eat so much fish.
6. Is there a lot of street food for sale _____ your town?

Confusing words: *food, meal, dish, plate*

> Remember that:
> - we use *food* to talk in general about things that people eat to keep them alive.
>   - ✓ *The most common food in Mongolia is meat.*
>   - ✗ *The most common meal in Mongolia is meat.*
> - we use *meal* to talk about an occasion when food is eaten or all the food that is eaten on such an occasion.
>   - ✓ *At weddings, there is usually a formal meal.*
>   - ✗ *At weddings, there is usually a formal food.*
> - we use *dish* to talk about food that is served in a particular way as part of a meal.
>   - ✓ *One of the main dishes in my country is pizza.*
>   - ✗ *One of the main plates in my country is pizza.*
> - we use *plate* to talk about a flat, usually round, object that you eat food from or serve food on.
>   - ✓ *What influences the food on your plate?*
>   - ✗ *What influences the food on your dish?*

3 Circle the correct option.

1. On the last day of our trip, we had a lovely Arabic food / **meal** in a traditional restaurant.
2. The restaurant offers a variety of delicious traditional **plates** / **dishes** to choose from.
3. I like vegetarian **meal** / **dishes** like risotto or a cheese omelette.
4. You must try the delicious Greek **food** / **meal** in Plaka's famous restaurants.
5. The accommodation includes two **foods** / **meals**: breakfast and dinner.
6. I really enjoy eating Japanese **meal** / **food**.

Speaking extra

Buying clothes

1 ★ ▶ 1.3 **Put the words in order to make sentences.**

1 pop / crazy / Mum / music / was / about
   _____
2 weren't / into / My / that / music / parents
   _____
3 disco / I / they / guess / liked
   _____
4 the Beatles / were / grandparents / into / My
   _____
5 into / My / Michael Jackson / both / parents / were / really
   _____
6 that / were / punk music / with it / They / went / and / into / everything
   _____

2 ★ 🔊 09 **Listen to the conversation. What is the relationship between the boy and the girl?**

3 ★★ 🔊 09 **Complete the conversation with the words in the box. Then listen again and check.**

| looks   changing   size   suits   fit   about |

Girl: So, you've got a pair of jeans. Let's find a cool T-shirt for you.
Boy: How ¹_____ this one? It's got a big green L on the front!
Girl: Yeah, L for 'loser'.
Boy: Hey! Come on, you're supposed to be helping me!
Girl: Here, try this one.
Boy: OK, where are the ²_____ rooms?
Girl: Over there. And try this one as well.
Boy: So what do you think?
Girl: Well, it doesn't ³_____ very well. It's too small for you.
Boy: But it's M – medium. It's my ⁴_____ .
Girl: Have you put on weight?
Boy: Very funny.
Girl: Sorry, but it ⁵_____ a bit tight.
Boy: I'll try the other one on.
Girl: OK, that's better. You look great in that one.
Boy: Do you think so? Do you think this colour ⁶_____ me?
Girl: Red? Of course … it goes with your red hair!
Boy: This is the last time I go shopping with my sister!

Pronunciation focus

4 ★ 🔊 10 **Listen to the sentences. Which words are stressed in each one? Listen and repeat.**

1 These shoes don't fit me.
2 I don't think it suits you.
3 You don't look good in that dress.
4 This coat is not my size.
5 I'm not so sure.

5 ★ 🔊 11 **Listen to the conversation. What is the problem with the second dress that Amy tries on?**

6 ★★★ 🔊 11 **Listen again and complete the conversation.**

Amy: Right, Sue, ¹_____ this dress for Sophie's party? I like the stripes.
Sue: Yeah, it's a nice dress. But stripy clothes don't ² _____ .
Amy: Yeah, you're right and it's a bit short, isn't it?
Sue: Hey, look at this one. It's denim but it's a lovely colour.
Amy: OK, I think I'll try it on.
³_____ ?
Sue: They're over there. I'll be there in a minute.
Sue: So, let's see you.
Amy: OK, here's the denim dress. What do you think?
Sue: Wow! ⁴_____ !
Amy: Do you think? I think it's too small.
Sue: No, it's definitely ⁵_____ . Not too big here not too small there!
Amy: Hold on, I've got another one.
Sue: Err … no, that doesn't ⁶_____ . It's really baggy.
Amy: What do you mean? It's perfect!
Sue: Yes, you're right. It's perfect. But Amy … it's the same dress I'm going to wear to Sophie's party. Sorry.

7 ★★ 🔊 11 **Listen again and check your answers. Then listen and repeat the conversation.**

Speaking extra   87

Speaking extra

Showing concern

1 ★ ▶ 2.3 Complete the sentences with the words in the box.

> come easier little difficult through helps

1. That seems to help a _____ .
2. I've helped my best friend Kate _____ a lot of things.
3. I can't say I've helped anyone through a _____ situation.
4. I'm a good listener, so my friends always _____ to me with their problems.
5. I've talked to him a lot on the phone and that _____ .
6. I hope that makes it a little _____ .

2 ★ 🔊 12 Listen to the conversation. What's Jo's problem?

3 ★★ 🔊 12 Complete the conversation with the words in the box. Then listen again and check.

> worry up mean poor better fine down

Tim: What's ¹_____ , Jo?
Jo: I told my dad I wanted to give up piano lessons and now he's angry with me.
Tim: Oh, you ²_____ thing! Why is he angry?
Jo: Well, you know my dad … he's so passionate about music.
Tim: Well, I'm sure he'll calm ³_____ soon. Why do you want to give up?
Jo: I don't know … it's just that we've got all these exams and I'm trying to study every day and I have piano lessons twice a week. And Chinese classes and hockey at the weekend.
Tim: I know what you ⁴_____ . It's really hard to do everything!
Jo: And I have to practise this really difficult piece on the piano. I just don't think I'm very talented when it comes to music.
Tim: Of course you are. You don't need to ⁵_____ . You're so hard-working. I'm sure you'll learn it.
Jo: But I have to play the whole thing tomorrow.
Tim: I'm sure it'll be ⁶_____ . Just keep practising. So, how can I make you feel ⁷_____ ?
Jo: Can you listen to me play it and tell me … honestly … what you think?
Tim: Of course, go on then.

Pronunciation focus

4 ★ 🔊 13 Listen to the sentences. Do they go up or down? Listen and repeat.
1. I'm sure it'll be fine.
2. You don't need to worry.
3. I know what you mean.
4. I'm sure she'll calm down soon.
5. Oh! You poor thing.

5 ★ 🔊 14 Listen to the conversation. What happened to Dylan's brother's guitar?

6 ★★★ 🔊 14 Listen again and complete the conversation.

Dylan: Lewis, you have to help me!
Lewis: OK, Dylan, ¹_____ ?
Dylan: Remember the other night at my house when I borrowed my brother's guitar?
Lewis: Yes, isn't it funny that I have the same guitar as your brother?
Dylan: Well, now there's a hole in the back of the guitar. He's really angry!
Lewis: Well, I'm sure ²_____ . I've got a hole in my guitar but it doesn't matter really. … That's funny, I can't find it now.
Dylan: But now he won't lend me his guitar.
Lewis: ³_____ . Do you want to borrow mine?
Dylan: Great thanks. But what about my brother?
Lewis: Oh, I'm sure he'll ⁴_____ .
Dylan: Yes, but he really loves that guitar.
Lewis: ⁵_____ make you feel better?
Dylan: I don't know … I hate it when I can't talk to my brother.
Lewis: I know ⁶_____ . It's awful.
Dylan: But how did I make a hole in the guitar?
Lewis: You ⁷_____ . He'll soon realise that … Hold on. This isn't my guitar. Look, the strings are different!
Dylan: That's my brother's guitar!
Lewis: And he has my guitar … the one with the hole!

7 ★★ 🔊 14 Listen again and check your answers. Then listen and repeat the conversation.

Speaking extra

Making decisions

1 ★ ▶ 3.3 **Join the parts of the sentences.**
1. My favourite band's going to be in town next month
2. I'm saving up for an electric guitar
3. I've seen a second-hand one that I really like
4. I also want to travel some before I start
5. I get money from doing chores around the house

a. but it's really expensive.
b. so I'm saving some of that to help pay for it.
c. and I don't want to miss that.
d. so I'm saving for that, too.
e. so I can play a wider range of songs.

2 ★ 🔊 15 **Listen to the conversation. What are they trying to decide?**

3 ★★ 🔊 15 **Complete the conversation with the words in the box. Then listen again and check.**

> suggest   way   need   shall   thinking   idea   rather

Girl: So, what are we going to buy Mum for her birthday?
Boy: Do we have to decide now? I'm in the middle of level 37 of this game!
Girl: Level 37? Wow! Anyway, yes, we ¹_____ to decide quickly because her birthday is next Saturday.
Boy: OK, well, I was ²_____ of a nice silk scarf or a bag, something like that.
Girl: But she's got lots of bags and I think Dad was going to buy her a really expensive one. I think I'd ³_____ buy her something really different – what about a ride in a fast car, like a Ferrari or a Lamborghini? You know she loves cars.
Boy: But isn't that really expensive?
Girl: It's not that expensive, and I think Gran and Granddad would help us.
Boy: Well, if they're going to help us, why don't we give her something really nice?
Girl: What kind of thing do you ⁴_____?
Boy: What about a weekend away in a nice hotel?
Girl: Yes, that's a good ⁵_____, too.
Boy: Sometimes I have good ideas, you know!
Girl: So how ⁶_____ we decide?
Boy: Hmm … good question. Hold on, I think the best ⁷_____ is to ask Mum – she's always good at choosing presents for people.
Girl: Yeah, but the present is for her!!!
Boy: Oh, yeah!!

Pronunciation focus

4 ★ 🔊 16 **Listen to the sentences. Which words are linked? Listen and repeat.**
1. I was thinking of buying her a scarf.
2. That's a good idea.
3. Personally, I'd rather go on a holiday.
4. I think the best way is to ask someone.
5. What kind of thing do you suggest?

5 ★ 🔊 17 **Listen to the conversation. What are Oliver and Emily going to talk about in the class presentation?**

6 ★★★ 🔊 17 **Listen again and complete the conversation.**

Oliver: So, we have to make a presentation to the class and we haven't even thought about what we're going to talk about.
Emily: I have thought about it. ¹_____ doing a presentation about interesting celebrations around the world.
Oliver: I think Conor and Natalie are going to do that. Personally, ²_____ talk about some different career possibilities in the future. We talked about it one day in social science class.
Emily: Oh yeah! ³_____ , too. But do you think it'll be easy to find information?
Oliver: Yes, actually, I've already done a bit of research and there's loads of stuff on the Internet.
Emily: OK, great. So ⁴_____ who does what. Someone has to write the presentation.
Oliver: And we should probably include some pictures.
Emily: OK, what kind of pictures ⁵_____ ?
Oliver: Hmm … I don't know. We can decide that when the time comes. ⁶_____ who does what, then?
Emily: ⁷_____ is for me to let you start and when it's ready I'll make the presentation.
Oliver: Ha ha. So I do all the work?
Emily: Of course.

7 ★★ 🔊 17 **Listen again and check your answers. Then listen and repeat the conversation.**

Speaking extra 89

Speaking extra

Giving instructions

1 ★ ▶ **4.3** Complete the sentences with the words in the box.

| skip   get up   vegetarian   choose   stand   dishes |

1 I'd cook on a Saturday so I wouldn't have to _____ so early.
2 If I could _____ the meal, I'd pick lunch.
3 We did cooking at school last year, so I can think of a lot of _____ .
4 I can't _____ cooking, so I'd ask my brother to write a menu.
5 I'd _____ breakfast since I never eat it anyway.
6 I'm a _____ , so that would be a problem with my family.

2 ★ 🔊 **18** Listen to the conversation. What are the girls making?

3 ★★ 🔊 **18** Complete the conversation with the words in the box. Then listen again and check.

| stir   thing   Finally   Next   Then   first |

Cerys: So, are you going to help me or not?
Sarah: Yes, of course. What do we need?
Cerys: OK, the first ¹_____ to do is get the ingredients. We'll need eggs, flour and sugar …
Sarah: … and butter and yoghurt from the fridge. Right. What's next?
Cerys: So, ²_____ of all, put the sugar and butter into a bowl and mix them together.
Sarah: OK, that's done. What now?
Cerys: Now break the eggs and mix those in.
Sarah: Yuk, it looks a bit slimy now.
Cerys: Well, you haven't finished yet. ³_____, you add the yoghurt. You need to ⁴_____ it a lot.
Sarah: If I had a machine, this would be easier.
Cerys: ⁵_____ all you do now is start mixing in the flour.
Sarah: Mmm … that's delicious.
Cerys: ⁶_____, when you've finished mixing it, put it in here and spread it out.
Sarah: Mmm … OK, hold on, just a little bit more.
Cerys: Come on. If you don't put it in the oven to bake now, you'll have nothing left!

Pronunciation focus

4 ★ 🔊 **19** Listen to the instructions. Do they go up or down? Which instruction goes down? Why? Listen and repeat.
1 First of all, mix the ingredients together.
2 Then, put it in the fridge for about 10 minutes.
3 Next, you spread the mix out in here.
4 Finally, put it in the oven for 20 minutes.

5 ★ 🔊 **20** Listen to the conversation. What are the boys making?

6 ★★★ 🔊 **20** Listen again and complete the conversation.

Jamie: So, do you remember how we made them the last time?
Paolo: Yes, of course I remember. It was really easy.
Jamie: Good, because you're going to make them this time. So what's first?
Paolo: Erm … the ¹_____ is to chop some onions and to fry them a little bit.
Jamie: Yes, that's right. Then what?
Paolo: ²_____ is to mix the other ingredients together.
Jamie: OK, so what are the other ingredients?
Paolo: Erm … minced meat, of course. And …
Jamie: … bread. Well, breadcrumbs. And one other thing.
Paolo: Eggs. So, ³_____ the minced meat, the bread and the eggs together.
Jamie: That's right. You need to ⁴_____ . Use your hands.
Paolo: ⁵_____ the fried onions.
Jamie: Yes. Don't forget to add salt and pepper.
Paolo: ⁶_____, when the mix is ready, I make some balls of meat and hit them with my hand to make them flat.

7 ★★ 🔊 **20** Listen again and check your answers. Then listen and repeat the conversation.

Language focus extra

Past simple vs. past continuous

1 Complete the sentences with the past simple or past continuous form of the verbs in brackets.
1. Mathew ___was playing___ (play) in the garden when he _____ (find) a gold coin.
2. Elena _____ (not hear) the teacher's question because she _____ (chat).
3. While we _____ (fish) last weekend, we _____ (catch) a large fish.
4. Lisa _____ (not see) the end of the film because she _____ (talk) on her phone.
5. They _____ (not go) out yesterday because it _____ (rain) all day.

Present perfect and past simple

2 Complete the email with the present perfect or past simple form of the verbs in brackets.

Hi Ollie,
How [1] ___were___ (be) your holidays? We [2] _____ (go) to Portugal for two weeks. We [3] _____ (cycle) along the coast and [4] _____ (eat) lots of delicious food! Term [5] _____ (begin) last Monday and I [6] _____ (start) at my new school. I [7] _____ (not be) here very long, but I love it! I [8] _____ (make) some new friends and I [9] _____ (join) the football team. I [10] _____ (not have) any homework back, but I hope they aren't too strict!
Your friend,
Lucy

Present perfect with *still*, *yet*, *already* and *just*

3 Circle the correct words.

A: Nick, have you finished your project [1]**still** / **yet**?
B: Yes, I've [2]**just** / **yet** finished!

C: I wrote to Mike this morning but he [3]**still** / **already** hasn't replied.
D: Well, maybe he hasn't checked his email [4]**yet** / **already**.

E: Have you eaten dinner [5]**still** / **yet**?
F: Yes. We eat early in our house – we've [6]**already** / **yet** finished!

Word order in questions

4 Circle the correct options.
1. You do / **Do you** go to school by bus?
2. What **is he** / **he is** doing tonight?
3. **Were they** / **They were** at home last night?
4. How long **did you** / **you did** live in France?
5. **Are you** / **You are** from Italy?

Subject/object questions

5 Write questions for these answers.
1. Who ___won first prize___ ?
   Sally won first prize.
2. Who _____ ?
   Rob sings the best.
3. What _____ ?
   They watched a football match.
4. Who _____ ?
   Their dad watched them play.
5. What _____ ?
   Music makes me happy.

Present perfect with *ever*, *never*, *for* and *since*

6 Complete the mini-conversations.

A: Have you [1] ___ever___ been to Australia?
B: No, but I've wanted to go [2] _____ I was a child.
A: Really? My aunt has lived there [3] _____ ten years – she loves it.

C: Have you [4] _____ played the violin?
D: Yes, I've had violin lessons [5] _____ I was ten.
C: Really! I've [6] _____ heard you play!

Present perfect questions

7 Write questions with the present perfect.
1. he / buy / the concert tickets / yet?
   Has he bought the concert tickets yet?
2. How long / he / live / in London?
   _____
3. they / take / their test / yet?
   _____
4. you / ever / go / Hawaii?
   _____
5. Where / she / go / for her holiday?
   _____

Language focus extra

used to and *would*

1 Rewrite the underlined phrases using *used to* or *would*. If both are possible, use *would*. If neither is possible, write ✗.

1. We <u>went</u> to the cinema every afternoon when I was young.
   would go
2. <u>Did you have</u> long hair when you were young?
   _____
3. I <u>saw</u> the Rolling Stones once in Hyde Park.
   _____
4. Where <u>did you live</u> when you were at college?
   _____
5. We <u>didn't have</u> a lot of money in those days.
   _____
6. They <u>sat</u> in coffee shops all day when they were students.
   _____
7. She <u>didn't eat</u> meat even when she was a child.
   _____
8. <u>Did you go</u> to the Isle of Wight Festival in 1980?
   _____

2 Complete the conversation with the correct form of *used to* or *would*. If both are possible, use *would*.

Julie: What kind of music ¹ _*did*_ you _*use to*_ like when you were younger?
Dad: Oh we ² _____ listen to all kinds of music. Your mother and I ³ _____ like soul and reggae.
Julie: Really? ⁴ _____ you _____ go to concerts together?
Dad: Oh yes, all the time! We ⁵ _____ hang out with the musicians after the concerts and we ⁶ _____ get home until 3 or 4 o'clock in the morning.
Julie: That sounds cool! How ⁷ _____ you _____ get home?
Dad: We ⁸ _____ have a car, so we ⁹ _____ walk all the way home hand in hand under the stars and we ¹⁰ _____ sing all our favourite songs.
Julie: That sounds romantic!

Past perfect

3 Complete the sentences with the correct form of the verbs in brackets. Use the past simple and the past perfect in each sentence.

1. Karen ___*went*___ (go) home because she ___*had forgotten*___ (forget) her ticket.
2. _____ you _____ (hear) of this band before we _____ (see) them last week?
3. We _____ (be) late for school because we _____ (miss) the early bus.
4. Hayley _____ (be) upset because they _____ (not invite) her to their party.
5. I only _____ (pass) my driving test after I _____ (take) it three times.
6. Sam _____ (play) with three different bands before he _____ (become) famous.
7. How many stories _____ you _____ (write) before you _____ (publish) your first book?
8. We _____ (go) to the Thai restaurant because _____ (not try) Thai food before.
9. _____ they _____ (climb) any mountains before they _____ (go) to Kilimanjaro?
10. How long _____ she _____ (live) in Japan before she _____ (meet) her boyfriend?

4 Complete the paragraph with the past simple or the past perfect form of the verbs in brackets.

Have you seen this photo? It's my aunt at Glastonbury 1992. It was the first time she ¹ ___*went*___ (go) to a music festival. She ² _____ (never/go) to Glastonbury before but she ³ _____ (always/want) to go and all her friends ⁴ _____ (have) a crazy time there the year before. Anyway, when she ⁵ _____ (get) there, the whole place ⁶ _____ (be) packed. She ⁷ _____ (never/see) so many tents before. Then she realised she ⁸ _____ (not bring) her tent! Luckily, her friends ⁹ _____ (arrive) the day before and they ¹⁰ _____ (set) up a large tent and she ¹¹ _____ (stay) there with them. They ¹² _____ (dance) to music all night long. It's strange – I can't imagine her at a festival, she's so serious nowadays!

Language focus extra

Reflexive pronouns and *each other*

1 Complete the sentences with reflexive pronouns or *each other*.

1 Maria introduced ____herself____ to her new classmates.
2 I often talk to _____ when I'm in the shower.
3 Can we help _____ to some more cake?
4 You need to prepare _____ for the test next week.
5 My brother hurt _____ when he was working in the garden.
6 My friends and I don't send _____ birthday cards anymore – we send emails.
7 This cooker turns _____ off when the clock rings.
8 My mum and dad really enjoyed _____ at our school concert.
9 My brother and I hadn't seen _____ for ages.
10 My sister taught _____ to play the saxophone.

2 Circle the correct words.

Dear Lisa,
I'm really enjoying ¹**myself**/ me at my new dance class. Last week, we were very busy preparing ²**ourselves / us** for the end-of-term performance. All our parents came and watched ³**ourselves / us** in a new dance performance. I had a solo. I have a large mirror at home so that I can see ⁴**myself / me** while I'm practising. The performance was on Saturday. My best friend took a video of ⁵**itself / it**. I told ⁶**myself / me** not to be nervous, but it's really difficult to stay calm – how do professional dancers keep ⁷**themselves / them** calm? Do you think they have a special technique to help ⁸**themselves / them** not to be nervous? Anyway, I can send ⁹**yourself / you** some photos! Please write with your news. We haven't seen ¹⁰**each other / ourselves** for ages – let's meet soon!
Love, Carmen

Present perfect simple

3 Complete the mini-conversations with the present perfect form of the verbs in brackets.

A: How many slices of cake ¹____have____ you ____eaten____ (eat) today?
B: I ²_____ (not have) many – only three slices including this one!
C: ³_____ you _____ (hear) of this film?
D: Of course! I think I ⁴_____ (see) it about five times. But I can watch it again, it's brilliant!

E: I ⁵_____ (play) this new computer game ten times. It's really popular!
F: Really? How many times ⁶_____ you _____ (win) so far?

G: Where's Suzie? I ⁷_____ (not see) her today.
H: I don't know. She ⁸_____ (be) absent for four days now.

I: ⁹_____ Jason _____ (finish) this book?
J: No, he ¹⁰_____ only _____ (read) three chapters.

Present perfect continuous

4 Complete the sentences with the present perfect continuous form of the verbs in the box.

| go ~~have~~ play read call collect take visit walk study |

1 How long ____have____ you ____been having____ guitar lessons? You're really good!
2 _____ Suzanna _____ Italian this year? Does she like it?
3 Jack and Harry _____ computer games in the library every Saturday.
4 Where _____ they _____ on Sunday afternoons? They're never home!
5 Why _____ you _____ to school every day? Don't you like the bus?
6 I _____ her on the phone all day but she doesn't answer!
7 _____ you _____ that new music blog? It's great!
8 We _____ photos of all the buildings in our town for our website.
9 Mel _____ the art museum every weekend to learn about art.
10 Our school _____ winter clothing for homeless people this winter.

Language focus extra 97

Language focus extra

be going to and present tenses for the future

1 Match the sentences (1–10) with the correct descriptions (A–C).
1. Martina is going to study medicine.
2. The summer holidays start next week!
3. We're going to play tennis every day.
4. I'm staying with my friend Gina this summer.
5. My art class finishes in September.
6. We're graduating in June.
7. I leave for Tokyo tomorrow morning.
8. They're going to have a party on Saturday.
9. We're going to a concert tomorrow.
10. I'm not going to come out tonight – I'm too tired.

A future intention   1 __ __ __
B future arrangement   __ __ __
C scheduled future event __ __ __

2 Circle the correct options.
This summer I ¹**'m going**/ 'll go on a tour of China with my family. We ²**'re visiting / visit** some friends of my parents who live in Beijing. First, we ³**'re staying / 're going to stay** with them for five days and after that we ⁴**'re taking / take** a bus tour to some ancient historic sites. Our flight ⁵**leaves / will leave** next Tuesday at 6 am (horribly early!) and it ⁶**arrives / is arriving** at 6 am the next day. I ⁷**'m going to learn / learn** some Chinese phrases before I go, and when I get back, I ⁸**'m going to apply / 'm applying** for a Chinese language course – everyone says it's the language of the future, not English! The course ⁹**starts / 's starting** in September and it ¹⁰**takes / is taking** one year. I'm really looking forward to our trip and to learning a new language and about a new culture!

Predictions with *be going to*, *will* and *may/might*

3 Complete the predictions with the correct form of the verbs in the boxes.

| need | ~~be~~ | give | become |
| break | lend | pass | miss |

[might / ~~be going to~~]

'I haven't brought a coat.' 'It's OK. It
¹ _isn't going to be_ cold. They said so on the radio.'
'Is it cold outside?' 'Yes, I think you
² _____ a coat later on.'

[might / will]

'I'm nervous about the exam.' 'Don't worry – I'm sure you ³_____ .'
'Can I carry those glasses for you?' 'Yes, but be careful – you ⁴_____ them.'

[be going to / might]

'Oh no! It's already too late – we
⁵_____ the train!'
'Do you think Daniel ⁶_____ us a lift in his car?' 'I'm not sure. I'll ask him.'

[may / will]

'I need to borrow some brown shoes.' 'Brooke has some. She ⁷_____ you hers.'
'Do you feel confident about the future?' 'Yes, totally. I ⁸_____ a millionaire before I'm 21!'

Future continuous

4 Write future continuous questions about the year 2030 with the prompts.
1. people / live / until they're 150?
   Will people be living until they're 150?
2. How / we / spend / our free time?
   _____
3. Where / people / go / on holiday?
   _____
4. What fashions / we / wear?
   _____
5. children / go / to school?
   _____
6. What type of food / people / eat?
   _____

5 Write answers to the questions in Exercise 4 using the future continuous.
1. Yes / They / live / until they're 150
   Yes, they will. They'll be living until they're 150.
2. People / not read / books anymore
   _____
3. Spaceships / take / people to Mars for their holidays
   _____
4. We / design / our own clothes on computers
   _____
5. No / Children / do / all their classes online
   _____
6. Restaurants / serve / seaweed instead of vegetables
   _____

Language focus extra

First conditional with *if*, *when* and *unless*

1 Circle the correct words.
1. I **'ll cook** / cook an omelette if you **are** / 'll be hungry.
2. If you **make** / don't make the toast, I **'ll cook** / cook the eggs.
3. The sauce will get thicker **unless** / when you **add** / 'll add the flour.
4. You won't get any dessert **unless** / if you **eat** / 'll eat all your vegetables.
5. I **'ll make** / make tea and coffee when the guests **arrive** / will arrive.
6. If we **eat** / 'll eat out tonight, I **won't** / don't have to cook dinner!
7. Mum **might make** / makes a chocolate cake for you unless / **if** you ask her nicely.
8. If you 'll hurry / **hurry** up, we **might get** / get to the fish and chip shop before it closes.

2 Complete the conversations with the missing words. Circle the correct options.

A
Clare: Would you like to come over for dinner tonight? I ¹___ pizza if you ²___ the dessert. How does that sound?
Rosie: Great! ³___ I have time, I ⁴___ some ice cream from the supermarket on the way.

1	a	make	b	'm making	c	'll make
2	a	brings	b	bring	c	'll bring
3	a	If	b	When	c	Unless
4	a	'll buy	b	'm buying	c	buy

B
Chris: Where do you want to sit? If we ¹___ a table by the window, we ²___ a great view.
Martina: Yes, but it ³___ not be so noisy if we ⁴___ here in the corner.

1	a	get	b	gets	c	'll get
2	a	have	b	'll have	c	're having
3	a	might	b	won't	c	is
4	a	're sitting	b	'll sit	c	sit

C
Joey: If I ¹___ butter to this recipe, do you think it ²___ better?
Mum: Definitely! But remember that it won't cook ³___ you ⁴___ up the heat.

1	a	add	b	'll add	c	'm adding
2	a	tastes	b	's tasting	c	'll taste
3	a	if	b	when	c	unless
4	a	'll turn	b	turns	c	turn

Second conditional with *could* and *might*

3 Write second conditional sentences with the prompts.
1. If / Suzanna / have / enough money / go / to expensive restaurants
   If *Suzanna had enough money, she'd go to expensive restaurants* .
2. Martin / could go / cycling in the park / not have / so much homework
   Martin _____ .
3. If / we / not be / so busy / might go / to the beach this weekend
   If _____ .
4. Sam and Christy / not ask / for help / unless / they / really need / it
   Sam and Christy _____ .
5. If / someone / give / me / a free ticket to any country / I / go / to Australia
   If _____ .
6. I / not eat / raw fish / unless / be / in a Japanese restaurant
   I _____ .

4 Write questions for these answers.
1. What *would you do if you didn't need to study this weekend* ?
   If I didn't need to study this weekend, I might go shopping, or I might watch a movie.
2. How _____ ?
   If we shared a bedroom, we'd argue every day.
3. How _____ ?
   If he didn't talk to me, I'd feel very sad.
4. What _____ ?
   If I could have any superpower, I'd like to be able to fly.
5. Where _____ ?
   If I could fly, I'd go to the moon.
6. Who _____ ?
   If I could meet any film star, I'd choose Johnny Depp.

Irregular verbs

infinitive	past simple	past participle
be	was/were	been
become	became	become
begin	began	begun
break	broke	broken
build	built	built
buy	bought	bought
catch	caught	caught
choose	chose	chosen
come	came	come
do	did	done
drink	drank	drunk
drive	drove	driven
eat	ate	eaten
fall	fell	fallen
feed	fed	fed
feel	felt	felt
find	found	found
fly	flew	flown
get	got	got
give	gave	given
go	went	gone
have	had	had
hear	heard	heard
keep	kept	kept
know	knew	known
learn	learnt/learned	learnt/learned
leave	left	left
lose	lost	lost
make	made	made
meet	met	met
pay	paid	paid
put	put	put
read	read	read
run	ran	run
say	said	said
see	saw	seen
send	sent	sent
sit	sat	sat
sleep	slept	slept
speak	spoke	spoken
spend	spent	spent
swim	swam	swum
take	took	taken
teach	taught	taught
tell	told	told
think	thought	thought
wear	wore	worn
win	won	won
write	wrote	written

Phonemic symbols

consonants

/p/	pencil
/b/	bag
/t/	town
/d/	day
/tʃ/	cheese
/dʒ/	juice
/k/	cake
/g/	get
/f/	food
/v/	very
/θ/	Thursday
/ð/	that
/s/	speak
/z/	zebra
/ʃ/	shoe
/ʒ/	usually
/m/	mum
/n/	name
/ŋ/	sing
/h/	house
/l/	like
/r/	red
/w/	water
/j/	you

vowels

/iː/	see
/ɪ/	sit
/ʊ/	book
/uː/	zoo
/e/	pen
/ə/	teacher
/ɜː/	bird
/ɔː/	boring
/æ/	that
/ʌ/	run
/ɑː/	car
/ɒ/	lost

diphthongs

/eɪ/	say
/ɪə/	hear
/ʊə/	pure
/ɔɪ/	enjoy
/əʊ/	know
/eə/	chair
/aɪ/	buy
/aʊ/	now

Thanks and acknowledgments

The authors and publishers would like to thank a number of people whose support has proved invaluable during the planning, writing and production process of this course.

We would like to thank Diane Nicholls for researching and writing the Get it right! pages and Ingrid Wisniewska for writing the Grammar extra section.

We would like to thank Tim Foster for bringing his warmth and experience to the project and for his reliable and keen-eyed editorial work.

We would also like to thank the teams of educational consultants, representatives and managers working for Cambridge University Press in various countries around the world.

The authors and publishers are grateful to the following contributors:

Blooberry: concept design
emc design limited: text design and layouts
QBS Learning: photo selection and cover design
DSound, Soundtracks Studios & Ian Harker: audio production

Development of this publication has made use of the Cambridge English Corpus (CEC). The CEC is a computer database of contemporary spoken and written English, which currently stands at over one billion words. It includes British English, American English and other varieties of English. It also includes the Cambridge Learner Corpus, developed in collaboration with the University of Cambridge ESOL Examinations. Cambridge University Press has built up the CEC to provide evidence about language use that helps to produce better language teaching materials.

The authors and publishers acknowledge the following sources of copyright material and are grateful for the permissions granted. While every effort has been made, it has not always been possible to identify the sources of all the material used, or to trace all copyright holders. If any omissions are brought to our notice, we will be happy to include the appropriate acknowledgements on reprinting.

p. 3 (CL): Getty Images/Heath Korvola; p. 3 (BR): Getty Images/Saša Prudkov; p. 4 (CR): Alamy/©Jan Wlodarczyk; p. 5 (BR): Getty Images/Hjalmeida; p. 8 (TR): Getty Images/Jay Blakesberg; p. 9 (TL): Getty Images/Wavebreak Media; p. 9 (BC): Getty Images/Peet Simard; p. 9 (BR): Alamy/©Kuttig - Travel; p. 10 (BL): Alamy/©Picture Partners; p. 11 (BL): Alamy/©Jamie Pham Photography; p. 12: Getty Images/Michael Ochs Archives/Stringer; p. 15 (BR): Shutterstock Images/Syda Productions; p. 17 (CR): Alamy/©Richard Levine; p. 19 (B): Alamy/©HelloWorld Images Premium; p. 20 (CR): Shutterstock Images/Joggie Botma; p. 21 (BL): Alamy/©Allan Zilkowsky; p. 22 (TR): Alamy/©Nico Smit; p. 27 (BL): Alamy/©National Geographic Image Collection; p. 28 (BL): Alamy/©Image Source; p. 29 (TL): Shutterstock Images/arek_malang; p. 29 (TR): Getty Images/Buda Mendes; p. 29 (CR): Getty Images/Udit Kulshrestha/Bloomberg; p. 29 (BR): Alamy/©Everett Collection Inc; p. 30 (CR): Getty Images/John Lamparski/WireImage; p. 30 (B/G): Shutterstock Images/Philip Birtwistle; p. 31 (T): Alamy/©Natalia Kuzmina; p. 31 (C): Shutterstock Images/Morrowind; p. 31 (B): Shutterstock Images/Bohbeh; p. 32 (CR): Getty Images/Bart Coenders; p. 35 (CR): REX/ITV; p. 37 (1): Shutterstock Images/Angelika Smile; p. 37 (2): Shutterstock Images/Ron Vargas; p. 37 (3): Getty Images/Clubfoto; p. 37 (4): Getty Images/Michael Powell; p. 37 (5): Getty Images/Daniel Loiselle; p. 37 (6): Getty Images/Ac_bnphotos; p. 37 (7): Alamy/©Ajcgoldberg/Stockimo; p. 37 (8): Shutterstock Images/NinaM; p. 37 (9): Alamy/©SoFood; p. 37 (10): Shutterstock Images/M. Unal Ozmen; p. 37 (TR): Alamy/©Jonathan Goldberg; p. 37 (CR): Shutterstock Images/Mariontxa; p. 37 (BR): Corbis/The food passionates; p. 38 (BL): Shutterstock Images/CandyBox Images; p. 38 (BC): Alamy/©a-plus image bank; p. 38 (TR): Getty Images/William Shaw; p. 38 (TC): Shutterstock Images/Foxy's Forest Manufacture; p. 38 (CR): Shutterstock Images/Roman Sigaev; p. 39 (1): Shutterstock Images/pavelgr; p. 39 (2): Shutterstock Images/dinsor; p. 39 (3): Getty Images/Doable/A.collection; p. 39 (4): Getty Images/Juanmonino; p. 39 (5): Shutterstock Images/Africa Studio; p. 39 (6): Alamy/©Radius Images; p. 39 (7): Getty Images/GooDween123; p. 39 (8): Getty Images/Paul Poplis; p. 39 (9): Shutterstock Images/Dulce Rubia; p. 39 (10): Alamy/©Mediablitzimages; p. 39 (CR): Getty Images/Jon Feingersh; p. 40 (CR): Alamy/©MBI; p. 41 (TL): Alamy/©Art Directors & TRIP; p. 42 (TL): Shutterstock Images/Martin Turzak; p. 47 (BL): Alamy/©Frances Roberts; p. 48 (CL): Shutterstock Images/David Pruter; p. 48 (C): Alamy/©Judith Collins; p. 49 (TL): Shutterstock Images/GoBOb; p. 49 (CR): Alamy/©Olivier Parent; p. 50 (CL): Getty Images/Peopleimages; p. 51 (T): Getty Images/Clark_fang; p. 51 (C): Shutterstock Images/Prapann; p. 51 (B): Alamy/©keith van-Loen; p. 54 (TC): Alamy/©ACE STOCK LIMITED; p. 54 (CR): Alamy/©Zoonar GmbH; p. 55: Shutterstock Images/Joe Seer; p. 57 (CR): Corbis/BEAWIHARTA/Reuters; p. 59 (T): Alamy/©Suzanne Long; p. 59 (BL): Getty Images/Scott Campbell/Contributor; p. 60 (BL): Getty Images/Henglein and Steets; p. 61 (1): Corbis/Ricardo Azoury; p. 61 (2): Getty Images/Jeff J Mitchell; p. 61 (3): Getty Images/Buda Mendes/LatinContent; p. 61 (4): Getty Images/Anna Bryukhanova; p. 61 (5): Getty Images/Jeff J Mitchell; p. 61 (6): Alamy/©Richard Levine; p. 62 (TR): Alamy/©Image Broker; p. 64 (TR): Alamy/©Tetra Images; p. 65 (BL): Alamy/©J.R. Bale; p. 67 (CR): Rex Features/Â©20thCentFox/Courtesy Everett C; p. 68 (TR): Getty Images/Larry Williams/LWA/Blend Images; p. 69 (TL): Shutterstock Images/Vadim Petrakov; p. 69 (CR): Getty Images/Alfred Eisenstaedt/Pix./The LIFE Picture Collection; p. 70 (TR): Getty Images/Harald Sund; p. 71 (T): Alamy/©Peter Polak; p. 71 (B): Shutterstock Images/Wavebreakmedia; p. 72 (T): Getty Images/David McNew; p. 74 (BL): Shutterstock Images/Vaclav Volrab; p. 75 (CL): Newscom/Aeromobil/SIPA; p. 77 (A): Alamy/©Kenny Williamson Glasgow; p. 77 (B): Alamy/©Peter Titmuss; p. 79 (TR): Alamy/©Steve Skjold; p. 81 (TL): Alamy/©Stockex; p. 81 (TR): Alamy/©Steve Mansfield-Devine; p. 82 (BL): Alamy/©Louise Heusinkveld; p. 87: Getty Images/Lisa Stirling; p. 88: Alamy/©Pere Sanz; p. 89: Alamy/©Ian Shaw; p. 90: Alamy/©Amana images inc.; p. 91: Alamy/©British Retail Photography; p. 92: Alamy/©IanDagnall Computing; p. 93: Getty Images/Rainer Elstermann; p. 94: Alamy/©JeffreyIsaacGreenberg.

Front cover photograph by Getty Images/Eduardo Garcia.

The publishers are grateful to the following illustrators:

Anni Betts p. 7; Q2A Media Services, Inc. p. 6, 11, 14, 21, 27, 41, 51, 52, 78, 79, 80.

CAMBRIDGE
UNIVERSITY PRESS

University Printing House, Cambridge CB2 8BS, United Kingdom

Cambridge University Press is part of the University of Cambridge.

It furthers the University's mission by disseminating knowledge in the pursuit of education, learning and research at the highest international levels of excellence.

www.cambridge.org
Information on this title: www.cambridge.org/9781107490475

© Cambridge University Press 2015

This publication is in copyright. Subject to statutory exception and to the provisions of relevant collective licensing agreements, no reproduction of any part may take place without the written permission of Cambridge University Press.

First published 2015
3rd printing 2016

Printed in Poland by Opolgraf

A catalogue record for this publication is available from the British Library

ISBN 978-1-107-46781-1 Student's Book with Online Workbook and Online Practice
ISBN 978-1-107-46780-4 Student's Book
ISBN 978-1-107-46782-8 Workbook with Online Practice
ISBN 978-1-107-49047-5 Combo A with Online Workbook and Online Practice
ISBN 978-1-107-49050-5 Combo B with Online Workbook and Online Practice
ISBN 978-1-107-46783-5 Teacher's Book
ISBN 978-1-107-46786-6 Audio CDs (3)
ISBN 978-1-107-46787-3 Video DVD
ISBN 978-1-107-49052-9 Presentation Plus DVD-ROM

Additional resources for this publication at www.cambridgelms.org/eyesopen

Cambridge University Press has no responsibility for the persistence or accuracy of URLs for external or third-party internet websites referred to in this publication, and does not guarantee that any content on such websites is, or will remain, accurate or appropriate. Information regarding prices, travel timetables, and other factual information given in this work is correct at the time of fi rst printing but Cambridge University Press does not guarantee the accuracy of such information thereafter.